CAMBRIDGE MUSIC HANDBOOKS

Britten: *War Requiem*

CAMBRIDGE MUSIC HANDBOOKS

GENERAL EDITOR Julian Rushton
Cambridge Music Handbooks provide accessible introductions to major
musical works.

Published titles

Bach: The Brandenburg Concertos MALCOLM BOYD
Bach: Mass in B Minor JOHN BUTT
Bartók: Concerto for Orchestra DAVID COOPER
Beethoven: Missa solemnis WILLIAM DRABKIN
Beethoven: Pastoral Symphony DAVID WYN JONES
Beethoven: Symphony No. 9 NICHOLAS COOK
Berg: Violin Concerto ANTHONY POPLE
Berlioz: Roméo et Juliette JULIAN RUSHTON
Brahms: A German Requiem MICHAEL MUSGRAVE
Britten: War Requiem MERVYN COOKE
Chopin: The Four Ballades JIM SAMSON
Debussy: La mer SIMON TREZISE
Handel: Messiah DONALD BURROWS
Haydn: The Creation NICHOLAS TEMPERLEY
Haydn: String Quartets, Op. 50 W. DEAN SUTCLIFFE
Holst: The Planets RICHARD GREENE
Ives: Concord Sonata GEOFFREY BLOCK
Janáček: Glagolitic Mass PAUL WINGFIELD
Liszt: Sonata in B Minor KENNETH HAMILTON
Mahler: Symphony No. 3 PETER FRANKLIN
Mendelssohn: The Hebrides and other overtures R. LARRY TODD
Mozart: Clarinet Concerto COLIN LAWSON
Mozart: The 'Jupiter' Symphony ELAINE R. SISMAN
Musorgsky: Pictures at an Exhibition MICHAEL RUSS
Schoenberg: Pierrot lunaire JONATHAN DUNSBY
Schubert: Die schöne Müllerin SUSAN YOUENS
Schumann: Fantasie, Op. 17 NICHOLAS MARSTON
Sibelius: Symphony No. 5 JAMES HEPOKOSKI
Strauss: Also sprach Zarathustra JOHN WILLIAMSON
Stravinsky: Oedipus rex STEPHEN WALSH
Verdi: Requiem DAVID ROSEN
Vivaldi: The Four Seasons and other concertos, Op. 8 PAUL EVERETT

Britten: *War Requiem*

Mervyn Cooke

Lecturer in Music
University of Nottingham

Published by the Press Syndicate of the University of Cambridge
The Pitt Building, Trumpington Street, Cambridge CB2 1RP
40 West 20th Street, New York, NY 10011-4211, USA
10 Stamford Road, Oakleigh, Melbourne 3166, Australia

First published 1996

Printed in Great Britain at the University Press, Cambridge

A catalogue record for this book is available from the British Library

Library of Congress cataloguing in publication data
Cooke, Mervyn.
Britten, War requiem / Mervyn Cooke.
p.   cm. – (Cambridge music handbooks)
Includes bibliographical references (p. 109) and index.
ISBN 0 521 44089 0 (hc). – ISBN 0 521 44633 3 (pb)
1. Britten, Benjamin, 1913–1976. War requiem.
I. Title.   II. Series.
ML410.B853C76   1996
782.32'38–dc20   96–6338   CIP

ISBN 0 521 44089 0 hardback
ISBN 0 521 44633 3 paperback

If in some smothering dreams you too could pace
Behind the wagon that we flung him in,
And watch the white eyes writhing in his face,
His hanging face, like a devil's sick of sin;
If you could hear, at every jolt, the blood
Come gargling from the froth-corrupted lungs,
Obscene as cancer, bitter as the cud
Of vile, incurable sores on innocent tongues, –
My friend, you would not tell with such high zest
To children ardent for some desperate glory,
The old Lie: Dulce et decorum est
Pro patria mori.

Wilfred Owen

Contents

Plates

Acknowledgements

I am indebted to the series editor, Professor Julian Rushton, for his constant encouragement and valuable suggestions; to Dr Philip Reed for his active participation in the project, which extended well beyond the confines of his textual contribution; to Dr Donald Mitchell for drawing my attention to much important documentary material; and to the staff of the Britten–Pears Library, Aldeburgh, for their customary helpfulness and freely shared expertise. At Cambridge University Press, thanks are due to Penny Souster for patiently overseeing the project, and to Peter Edwards.

Musical examples from the published scores of the *War Requiem* are © 1962 by Boosey & Hawkes (Music Publishers) Ltd, and reproduced here by their kind permission. The texts of Wilfred Owen's poems appear by permission of Chatto & Windus Ltd and the Estate of Wilfred Owen. All quotations from Britten's correspondence and unpublished manuscript sketches are © 1996 by the Trustees of the Britten–Pears Foundation, and appear by permission; these are not to be further reproduced without prior written permission from the Trustees. I am grateful to the Trustees of the Britten–Pears Library for permission to reproduce Plates 1 and 2.

The following library *sigla* are used in Chapter 2:

GB–ALb   The Britten–Pears Library, Aldeburgh
GB–Lbl   The British Library, London.

Owen, Britten and pacifism

At twelve noon on 11 November 1918, while bands played and bells rang as the crowds gathered to celebrate the Armistice which had just brought the First World War to a close, a telegram arrived at the home of Tom and Susan Owen in Shrewsbury. It informed them that their son, Lt Wilfred Edward Salter Owen MC, serial number 4756, had been killed in action in the early morning of 4 November while helping his troops to cross the Sambre Canal near Ors in north-east France. He was twenty-five years of age, and the news of his death had taken exactly one week to reach England.

The death of any soldier in action so close to the cessation of hostilities acquires a special poignancy, but Lt Owen had been no ordinary officer. He left behind him a small body of poetry, the finest examples of which – written during the last two years of the long and bloody war – make a passionate and eloquent outcry against man's inhumanity to man as he had witnessed it played out on the mud-drenched fields of Flanders. The vividness of Owen's trench scenes, coupled with a formidable poetic technique uniting verbal economy and emotional profundity, have assured him an enduring posthumous reputation as the greatest of the First World War poets. It was logical, therefore, that Benjamin Britten should have chosen in 1960 to set nine of Owen's finest war poems in his *War Requiem*, juxtaposing them with the Latin Mass for the Dead to create a unique pacifist statement fully in keeping with the composer's lifelong hatred of the violence and destruction of warfare.

Britten's pacifist inclinations are well known, and are discussed on pp. 11–19 below. Owen too, perhaps partly because of the association with Britten which the phenomenal success of the *War Requiem* has brought to his war poetry, has been seen in some quarters as the archetypal pacifist poet. But was Owen really a 'pacifist' in Britten's understanding of the word? Britten's pacifism, largely because of his firm refusal to fight in the Second World War, is far clearer-cut than that of Owen, who had himself made an equally firm decision to take an active part in the fighting. (Such is the emotive power of Owen's anti-war poetry that it has become necessary to remind ourselves that he was not conscripted.) The complexity of Owen's changing attitudes to both war and religion raises a number of conflicting issues of great relevance to Britten's own interpretation of Owen's poetry as revealed by his treatment of it in the *War Requiem*.

As was to be the case with Britten, the domineering influence in Owen's upbringing had been that of his mother. Susan Owen was a woman of formidable evangelical fervour with a strong streak of puritanism who, like Britten's mother, expected great things from her talented son from a tender age. Born in 1893 and the eldest of four children, Wilfred grew up to share his mother's religious and literary interests: indeed, the latter were kindled with a strength analogous to Britten's mother's cultivation of her son's musicality. The possessiveness of Wilfred's mother caused something of a rift in the Owen family, with the intellectual Wilfred becoming increasingly distanced from his down-to-earth father, while his rebellious younger brother Harold sided with their father and pursued the nautical career he had wished for all his sons.[1] Failing to enter university with the ease he had anticipated, Wilfred opted to work as an unpaid lay assistant in the parish of Dunsden (near Reading) in 1911, and there the stuffy atmosphere soon began to smother the fervent evangelism he had shared with his mother as a teenager. Writing to his sister Mary from Dunsden on 1 February 1913, he declared that 'no religion is worth the having', while recognizing the value of Christian spirits 'independent of what man can do unto them, either for evil or good'.[2] Less than a week later, he left Dunsden permanently. Seven months later he had moved to France to teach English in Bordeaux.

The most intriguing aspect of Owen's increasing antipathy towards conventional religion is his dissatisfaction with the mechanisms of liturgy and ritual, the complacency of which Britten also sharply criticizes by effective textual juxtapositions in the *War Requiem*. Owen highlighted the impersonality of orthodox worship in the poem 'Maundy Thursday', probably written in France during 1915 and among the best of his early writings:

> Above the crucifix I bent my head:
> The Christ was thin, and cold, and very dead:
> And yet I bowed, yea, kissed – my lips did cling
> (I kissed the warm live hand that held the thing.)

That same Easter, Owen had written to his mother from Merignac to say:

It is Easter Sunday morning, and we have just come back from High Mass: real, genuine Mass, with candle, with book, and with bell, and all like abominations of desolation: none of your anglican simulacrums. On Good Friday I went also. Always I come out from these performances an hour and a half older: *otherwise unchanged*.[3]

The futility of conventional religion in atoning for the sin of warfare is suggested by the overtly ecclesiastical imagery of 'Anthem for Doomed Youth', Britten's setting of which is provocatively placed soon after the beginning of the *War Requiem*.

Fourteen months elapsed between the declaration of war on 4 August 1914 and Owen's decision to enlist in the autumn of 1915, and during this period his letters home from France begin to show a developing awareness of the international and humanitarian issues involved in the conflict. One week after the outbreak of war, he wrote to his brother Colin and echoed a stereotyped sentiment prevalent at this early stage in the hostilities:

After all my years of playing soldiers, and then of reading History, I have almost a mania to be in the East, to see fighting, and to serve. For I like to think this is the last War of the World! I have only a faint idea of what is going on, and what is felt, in England.[4]

In a postscript to the same letter, Owen added 'Down with the Germans!' His poetic expression of warlike sentiments at this time is dramatically opposed to his later outlook, and a poem originally entitled 'The Ballad of Peace and War' (probably written in late 1914) provides a striking contrast to the later and considerably better-known outcry in 'Dulce et Decorum Est':

> O meet it is and passing sweet
> To live in peace with others,
> But sweeter still and far more meet
> To die in war for brothers.[5]

A visit in September 1914 to a Bordeaux hospital, where Owen could see for himself the horrific wounds inflicted on both French and German troops, immediately softened his attitude; but November saw him first thinking of the possibility of enlisting himself. He wrote to his mother: 'It is a sad sign if I do: for it means that I shall consider the continuation of my life of no use to England.'[6]

Although several important English writers (including Bertrand Russell and Lytton Strachey[7]) were already pacifists or conscientious objectors, it was a meeting with the influential French poet Laurent Tailhade at about this time which first seems to have opened Owen's mind to the cause of pacifism. The Frenchman had published two controversial pamphlets on pacifist themes (*Lettre aux conscrits* in 1903 and *Pour la paix* six years later), but opted to 'shoulder a rifle'[8] in 1914 at the age of fifty-nine, a development which must have done little to help Owen make his decision whether or not to fight. In December 1914 Owen first became painfully aware of the now legendary hostility in England directed against young men who refused to wage war for their country. A typical example was the statement by 'A Little Mother' whose letter to the *Morning Post* declaring that 'we women, who demand to be heard, will tolerate no such cry as "Peace! Peace!!" where there is no peace' was reprinted as a pamphlet and allegedly sold 75,000 copies in one week of circulation. Owen's comments on the subject to his mother have much in common with Britten's later attitude towards conscientious objection:

The *Daily Mail* speaks very movingly about the 'duties shirked' by English young men. I suffer a good deal of shame. But while those ten thousand lusty louts go on playing football I shall go on playing with my little axiom: – that my life is worth more than my death to Englishmen.

Do you know what would hold me together on a battlefield?: The sense that I was perpetuating the language in which Keats and the rest of them wrote! I do not know in what else England is greatly superior, or dearer to me, than another land and people.

Write immediately what I am to do.[9]

The turning-point was to come in June the following year, when Owen decided to take a commission in the Artists' Rifles, having toyed also with the possibility of joining the Italian Cavalry 'for reasons both aesthetic and practical'.[10] He told his mother: 'I don't want the bore of training, I don't want to wear khaki; nor yet to save my honour before inquisitive grand-children fifty years hence. But I *now do* most *intensely want to fight.*'[11]

Owen joined the Artists' Rifles on 21 October 1915 and, after basic training, was commissioned into the Manchester Regiment in June 1916. Further training followed before he finally entered active service, embarking for his first base camp at Etaples on 29 December and assuming command of 3 Platoon, A Company, in the Second Battalion of the Manchesters on the Somme in January 1917. He fought continuously (apart from a brief hospitalization for concussion) until falling victim to shell-shock in May, whereupon he returned to England for rehabilitation at the Craiglockhart War Hospital near Edinburgh. During his four months of recuperation at this convalescent home for neurasthenics, his outlook on both poetry and war rapidly matured through the friendship and mutual admiration he established with the poet Siegfried Sassoon, who was also a patient at

Craiglockhart. Owen's poetry had been up to this point thoroughly Keatsian in structure and subject-matter,[12] and he had received encouragement and criticism from Harold Monro shortly before joining up.[13] Shelley, too, had been a strong influence, especially in developing Owen's interest in pararhyme: it was Shelley's poem *The Revolt of Islam* which provided both the title and the theme for Owen's later masterpiece 'Strange Meeting' (the centrepiece of the final movement of the *War Requiem*).[14] But it was only with his inspirational exposure to Sassoon's outspoken views and poetical expertise that Owen's poetry began to achieve tangible mastery.

Like Owen, Sassoon reached full maturity in his poetry only when directly confronted with the horrors of war. Posted to France, but not yet in action, Sassoon met his fellow poet Robert Graves at Béthune in November 1915. Graves had been fighting since the spring, and showed Sassoon a draft of his first collection of poems: Sassoon 'frowned and said that war should not be written about in such a realistic way... I told him, in my old-soldier manner, that he would soon change his style.'[15] Graves's comment proved to be prophetic, and Sassoon soon became renowned as a war writer cultivating vivid realism. By the time he met Owen in Edinburgh, he had already published poems in the overtly pacifist *Cambridge Magazine* – the offices of which were ransacked by patriotic Royal Flying Corps cadets.

Writing to his mother from Craiglockhart on 15 August 1917, Owen commented:

I have just been reading Siegfried Sassoon, and am feeling at a very high pitch of emotion. Nothing like his trench life sketches has ever been written or ever will be written. Shakespere [*sic*] reads vapid after these. Not of course because Sassoon is a greater artist, but because of the subjects, I mean...

I have not yet dared to go up to him and parley in a casual way. He is here you know because he wrote a letter to the Higher Command which was too plain-spoken.[16]

Sassoon had arranged for a question to be asked in the House of Commons during the previous July on his belief 'that this war, upon which I entered as a war of defence and liberation, has now become a war of aggression and conquest'. He argued that 'the war is being deliberately prolonged by those who have the power to end it', and concluded his statement with the words

On behalf of those who are suffering now I make this protest against the deception which is being practised on them; also I believe that I may help to destroy the callous complacence with which the majority of those at home regard the continuance of agonies which they do not share, and which they have not sufficient imagination to realize.[17]

Sassoon, who held the rank of captain, ran the risk of court martial in making this bold stand against aggression, and as he had been shot in the chest his physical and mental well-being already left much to be desired. Graves (who was also encouraging Owen's poetical aspirations at this time) intervened to avert impending disaster, persuading the War Office to send Sassoon to Craiglockhart (or 'Dottyville', as Sassoon came to call it) for further medical attention and thereby draw a veil over their public embarrassment. As Ivor Gurney put it, 'they solved it in a becoming official fashion, and declared him mad, and put him in a lunatic-asylum'.[18] Before he went to Edinburgh, Sassoon threw his Military Cross into the sea. The decoration had been awarded for his rescue of a wounded man from a mine crater near enemy lines. Early in 1917 he was also recommended for the Victoria Cross (the highest military decoration) when, having been shot, he continued fighting; the award was declined because the action had proved unsuccessful. In every way 'Mad Jack' Sassoon was a war-hero of the kind the British Government longed for, and it was his voice they chose to silence. After his 'convalescence' at Craiglockhart, Sassoon again returned to active service (his poem 'When I'm asleep, dreaming and lulled and warm' tells how his conscience was pricked by the ghosts of old soldiers criticizing his absence), and he later survived a bullet wound to the head. Like Owen, he felt the need to participate actively in the conflict in order that his pacifist statements were seen to be beyond reproach.[19]

Sassoon's defiance helped Owen to formalize his own pacifist views, and these differ from Britten's later stance in one crucial respect: both Sassoon and Owen had been prepared to fight in the name of 'defence and liberation', but not to further the aggression of their own nation. This is the message Owen was to express so succinctly in the concluding sestet of the sonnet 'The Next War' (set by Britten as part of the 'Dies irae' of the *War Requiem*):

> Oh, Death was never enemy of ours!
> We laughed at him, we leagued with him, old chum.
> No soldier's paid to kick against his powers.
> We laughed, knowing that better men would come,
> And greater wars; when each proud fighter brags
> He wars on Death – for lives; not men – for flags.

In June 1917 Owen had told his mother that his aim in war was the 'Extinction of Militarism beginning with Prussian'[20] and, responding to a

6

statement by H. G. Wells in the *Daily Mail* on 22 August which called for peace between belligerents and pacifists and the defeat of 'militant imperialism', Owen declared:

As for myself, I hate washy pacifists as temperamentally as I hate whiskied prussianists. Therefore I feel that I must first get some reputation of gallantry before I could successfully and usefully declare my principles.[21]

In the mean time, Owen could do no better than to compensate for the home front's lack of 'imagination' by adopting Sassoon's vivid style in his own war poetry, beginning with 'The Dead-Beat', written in excited haste immediately after the first encounter between the two poets. Sassoon continued to encourage him in his creative writing, and suggested Owen adopt the highly appropriate title 'Anthem' for his sonnet 'Anthem for Doomed Youth' – a poem which, along with 'The Next War', he described as 'my two best war Poems'.[22]

Owen's increasingly pacifist inclinations formed the last remaining link with his earlier strictly religious upbringing. Writing to his mother in May 1917 he stated:

Although I have comprehended a light which never will filter into the dogma of any national church: namely that one of Christ's essential commands was: Passivity at any price! Suffer dishonour and disgrace; but never resort to arms. Be bullied, be outraged, be killed; but do not kill.[23]

He added 'am I not a conscientious objector with a very seared conscience?' and concluded his observations on the subject with the following remark: 'Thus you see how pure Christianity will not fit in with pure patriotism.' But his ideas were still far from inflexible, and some three months later he wrote again to his mother in terms which constitute a conscious turning against his earlier biblical exemplar:

While I wear my star and eat my rations, I continue to take care of my Other Cheek; and, thinking of the eyes I have seen made sightless, and the bleeding lad's cheeks I have wiped, I say: Vengeance is mine, I, Owen, will repay.[24]

In this more defiant spirit, his ideas on pacifism still confused, Owen returned to active service on the Somme in August 1918 after eight months of military duties in England.

Not surprisingly, antipathy towards religion was widespread in the trenches. Graves noted that 'hardly one soldier in a hundred was inspired by religious feeling of even the crudest kind', and attributed much of the fighting man's scorn for the Church to the rule which forbade Anglican chaplains to risk their lives at the front line.[25] Praising mankind's resilience and (like many others) expressing theological scepticism arising from God's refusal to intervene and prevent bloody conflicts, Gurney commented that 'the contrast between the magnificent behaviour of Man to that of the apparent callousness of God is most striking... [God's] debt to Europe, to the world, is very great'.[26] This irony surfaces in Owen's poem 'Soldier's Dream', written between October 1917 and the following summer:

> I dreamed kind Jesus fouled the big-gun gears;
> And caused a permanent stoppage in all bolts;
> And buckled with a smile Mausers and Colts;
> And rusted every bayonet with His tears.
>
> And there were no more bombs, of ours or Theirs,
> Not even an old flint-lock, nor even a pikel.
> But God was vexed, and gave all power to Michael;
> And when I woke he'd seen to our repairs.

His feelings on the subject were clarified in 'The Parable of the Old Man and the Young' (set by Britten in the 'Offertorium') where Abraham's refusal to sacrifice the 'Ram of Pride' results in the death of his son and 'half the seed of Europe'. In 'At a Calvary near the Ancre' (the focal text of Britten's 'Agnus Dei'), pride is again viewed as man's principal failing and the conclusion takes the pacifist standpoint to its ultimate extreme:

> But they who love the greater love
> Lay down their Life; they do not hate.

On the other hand, patriotism was treated just as cynically in the trenches as religious sentiment, being 'rejected as fit only for civilians, or prisoners. A new arrival who talked patriotism would soon be told to cut it out.'[27] All in all, the common soldier at the front line remained remarkably neutral in outlook and even retained fraternal feelings towards his enemy, as described by Gurney: 'In the mind of all the English soldiers I have met there is absolutely no hate for the Germans, but a kind of brotherly though slightly contemptuous kindness – as to men who are going through a bad time as well as themselves... The whole thing is accepted as a heavy Burden of Fate.'[28] This sense of paradoxical fraternization is the starting-point for Owen's 'Strange Meeting'.

No pacifist sentiments are to be found in the letters Owen wrote during the last two months of fighting before his death. In addition, it is interesting to note that the humanitarian arguments quoted above are exclusively to be found in correspondence dating from his year of convalescence in the United Kingdom. It is perhaps not surprising that letters written home while on active service do not contain comments which could be misinterpreted as symptomatic of cowardice: Owen was himself responsible for censoring outgoing letters written by the men in his charge and had to set an impeccable example, although he did relax his principles by employing a secret code in his own letters to inform his mother of the exact location of the battalion at the time of writing.[29] From the moment he joined up, his letters had frequently revealed a grim sense of humour (no doubt a defence mechanism) which made light of his perils. In July 1915, for instance, he had quipped 'It takes a lot to give me a headache; – let's hope it won't need a bullet!' and shortly after he started fighting he reported excitedly: 'This morning I was hit! We were bombing and a fragment from somewhere hit my thumb knuckle. I coaxed out 1 drop of blood. Alas! no more!!'[30] It is disconcerting to find the 'pacifist' poet plundering a German Albatross biplane which crashed near his position on 8 April 1917 and retaining the dead pilot's bloodstained handkerchief as a souvenir, or ensuring he remembered to send his brother Colin 'some loot, from a pocket which I rifled on the Field'.[31] Such unsentimental realities of war were not, it is interesting to note, recounted by Owen in letters to his mother.

Owen's courage on active service was officially recognized by the award of the Military Cross for 'conspicuous gallantry and devotion to duty in the attack on the Fonsomme Line on 1st/2nd October 1918'.[32] Again, it is paradoxical to read in the official citation that Owen inflicted considerable casualties on the enemy with the German machine-gun he had captured single-handedly. Owen told the story in his own words in a discreetly toned-down version contained in a letter home, written immediately after the incident and marked 'Strictly private' (i.e. not to be shown to anyone outside his closest family):

I lost all my earthly faculties, and fought like an angel.

If I started into detail of our engagement I should disturb the censor and my own Rest.

You will guess what has happened when I say I am now Commanding the Company, and in the line had a boy lance-corporal as my Sergeant-Major.

With this corporal who stuck to me and shadowed me like your prayers, I captured a German Machine Gun and scores of prisoners.

I'll tell you exactly how another time. I only shot one man with my revolver (at about 30 yards!); The rest I took with a smile...

I came out in order to help these boys – directly by leading them as well as an officer can; indirectly, by watching their sufferings that I may speak of them as well as a pleader can. I have done the first.[33]

Exactly one month later, while helping to lay duckboards at the bank of the Sambre Canal, Wilfred Owen was shot dead.

Owen's final assessment of his achievements is modest, for the body of poetry which became his legacy to posterity truly speaks of the suffering he had witnessed in the trenches. Here, far more than in his often self-conscious letters to his family, does the profundity of his abhorrence of warfare shine through. Yet his poetic maturity came too late for him to have seen more than a handful of his poems in print.[34] While retraining at Scarborough in 1918 he had drawn up a draft list of poems to be included in a first collection under the provisional title 'Disabled & Other Poems', sketching out the famous Preface which Britten selectively quotes on the title-page of the *War Requiem* and which has become the poet's most celebrated summary of his literary and humanitarian aims:

This book is not about heroes. English poetry is not yet fit to speak of them.

Nor is it about deeds, or lands, nor anything about glory, honour, might, majesty, dominion, or power, except War.

Above all I am not concerned with Poetry.

My subject is War, and the pity of War.

The Poetry is in the pity.

Yet these elegies are to this generation in no sense consolatory. They may be to the next. All a poet can do today is warn. That is why the true Poets must be truthful.

(If I thought the letter of this book would last, I might have used proper names; but if the spirit of it survives – survives Prussia – my ambition and those names will have achieved themselves fresher fields than Flanders...)

Even here, with Owen's specific hope that the spirit of his work will survive Prussia, the emphasis suggests anti-militarism rather than unqualified pacifism. The poet's pacifist stance was never fully clarified, and the strength of his poetry lies more in compassion than conscientious objection. Indeed, his apparent inability to find a simple explanation for his own mixed feelings about the horrors of war prevents his poetic utterances from ever falling into the trap of dogmatism. His internal conflict is perhaps one 'every honest poet must face under the conditions of modern total war; for, if he refuse to take any part in it, he is opting out of the human condition and thus, while obeying his moral conscience, may well be diminishing himself as a poet'.[35]

The stupefying atrocities perpetrated by Hitler's Government during the

Second World War, whether genocidal or imperialistic in intent, provided for many an overwhelmingly persuasive reason to resort to arms once again. Even though the full extent of the Nazi barbarities was revealed only after the event, the crusade to liberate the oppressed from the yoke of fascism must in itself have seemed a much clearer-cut justification for war than any argument advanced in the politically complex turmoil of the First World War. In any case, by the summer of 1940 it had become abundantly clear that Hitler intended to mount an invasion of Britain: and to elect not to fight in direct defence of one's homeland put the next generation of conscientious objectors in an unenviable position. Even Owen and Sassoon had felt war to be admissible when its goals were 'defence and liberation'.

Although Britten's pacifist tendencies did not crystallize into a coherent viewpoint until the war was well under way, there had been many indications in earlier years of an incipient revulsion against inhumanitarian practices. In 1971 he recalled how he loathed the concept of corporal punishment at English schools,[36] and his hatred for the sadism it implied was later fully shown by the sympathetic treatment of the Novice after his brutal flogging in *Billy Budd* (1951). Shortly before leaving his own preparatory school in July 1928 he was awarded no marks for an essay on the subject of 'Animals' in which he expressed his loathing for cruelty in general and bloodsports in particular. When he became a pupil at Gresham's School, he declined to join the Officers' Training Corps. In 1935 Britten took part in door-to-door leaflet distribution for the pacifist cause in Lowestoft, and his private composition teacher Frank Bridge discussed his own pacifist beliefs with him: Britten wrote in his diary on 3 February 1935 that they pursued a 'very serious and interesting argument' on the topic. The issue of bloodsports surfaced again in *Our Hunting Fathers* (1936) where the hawks' names 'German' and 'Jew' are pointedly juxtaposed as a reminder of the disturbing escalation of Hitler's anti-Semitism.

The composite text for *Our Hunting Fathers* was created by W. H. Auden, who had already collaborated with Britten at the GPO Film Unit. Auden's influence undoubtedly helped to bring out the latent left-wing tendencies in Britten's political thinking at this time, but Auden was decidedly no pacifist and later wrote: 'I have absolutely no patience with Pacifism as a political movement, as if one could do all the things in one's personal life that create wars and then pretend that to refuse to fight is a sacrifice and not a luxury.'[37] But others of Britten's associates in his work for both the Film Unit and the politically outspoken Group and Left Theatres did not share Auden's views, and Christopher Isherwood (who co-authored with Auden the two plays *The*

Ascent of F6 and *On the Frontier* for which Britten provided incidental scores in 1937–8) was a noted pacifist.

Britten's first public acknowledgement of his pacifism came in March 1936 when he provided a short musical score for the controversial film *Peace of Britain*, directed by Paul Rotha for Freenat Films (the film unit of the League of Nations, also supported on this occasion by the TUC).[38] Although the film lasted only three minutes, its message of anti-rearmament was so politically sensitive that it was at first refused certification. Britten wrote in his diary on 8 April: 'The fuss caused by the Censor not passing that little Rotha Peace film is colossal. $\frac{1}{2}$ centre pages of Herald & News Chronicle, & Manchester Guardian – BBC. News twice. Never has a film had such good publicity!' The restriction was relaxed and certification was granted on the following day. Early in 1937, Britten collaborated with Ronald Duncan on a *Pacifist March* for the Peace Pledge Union, an organization committed (unlike the League of Nations) to total pacifism.[39] Duncan, who was to become the librettist of *The Rape of Lucretia* in 1946, published a pamphlet entitled *The Complete Pacifist* and lent Britten a copy of Richard Gregg's book *The Power of Non Violence* (London, 1935) 'which influenced him considerably'.[40] Duncan registered as a conscientious objector during the war, but since he was a farmer (an occupation deemed by the Government to be in the national good) he encountered few of the difficulties later to be borne by Britten.

By the end of 1936 Auden had decided to participate actively in the Spanish Civil War as an ambulance driver, Britten writing in his diary on 1 December: 'I try to dissuade him, because what the Spanish Gov. might gain by his joining is nothing compared with the world's gain by his continuing to write' (a sentiment with which Wilfred Owen would have concurred). On 8 January 1937, the day before the poet's departure, the two men met in London and Auden wrote out the poem 'It's farewell to the drawing-room's civilised cry' in a copy of Britten's *Sinfonietta*. Britten was to set this text to music two years later as part of the cantata *Ballad of Heroes* he composed for the festival of 'Music for the People' at the Queen's Hall, London, in early 1939. Intended to commemorate the fallen heroes of the International Brigade's British Battalion who fought in Spain, the libretto for the *Ballad* was compiled by the left-wing activist Randall Swingler. Many musical techniques and rhetorical gestures in the *Ballad* directly foreshadow those employed in the *War Requiem* over twenty years later – most strikingly in the dramatic spatial separation of the militaristic trumpet fanfares performed from the gallery.[41] Britten's pacifist inclinations had already been voiced in the text of his Whitsuntide radio project *The World of the Spirit* (compiled by R. Ellis Roberts), broadcast by the BBC on 5 June 1938: the narrated sections include accounts of William Penn's 'Treaty of Amity' with the American Indians ('It is not our custom to use hostile weapons against our fellow-creatures, for which reason we have come unarmed'), the story of a rabbi in the trenches of the First World War who secured a crucifix for a Roman Catholic soldier *in extremis* shortly before being killed himself by an exploding shell, and the execution of the Irish rebel James Connolly who declared 'You can shoot me if you like, but I am dying for my country.' In *The Company of Heaven*, an earlier radio cantata (29 September 1937) which had formed the model for *The World of the Spirit*, Britten's setting of a text from the Book of Revelation describing the war in heaven between Michael and the fallen angels incorporates music of considerable violence; as Donald Mitchell has pointed out, the powerful timpani writing looks directly ahead to the Wordsworth setting describing insomnia induced by reflection on the September massacres of the French Revolution in the *Nocturne* (1958), and to certain martial passages in the *War Requiem*.

By the time *Ballad of Heroes* was given its first performance in April 1939, Auden had already been in the United States for three months in the company of Isherwood. Britten's decision to cross the Atlantic with Peter Pears that same May was no doubt partly influenced by the earlier emigration of their associates. War, although imminent, had not yet been declared and Britten's pacifist views were still far from clarified. Settled in New York and befriended by Aaron Copland, Britten shared his fears with the American composer. Copland urged him not to return to the United Kingdom, but other friends were less sympathetic: at exactly this time Britten received a letter from Lennox Berkeley (written on 3 September, the day war was declared) which said 'I've always been a pacifist at heart, how can one be anything else? But I think if there ever was a case where force has got to be used, this is it.'[42] Although Berkeley urged Britten to continue composing, much in the same spirit as the latter had earlier encouraged Auden to write rather than fight, Britten took the comments badly and (his mood doubtless soured by the deteriorating personal relationship between them) declared that Berkeley was the 'only person who wrote to me about "duty", "conscience" – "being a pacifist at heart, but this was a war", etc. . . . – (sic, sic SIC!!!)'.[43]

The strongest musical expression of Britten's anxieties during his American years is to be found in the *Sinfonia da Requiem*, a work of complex significance, being partly an official commission, partly a personal *envoi* to the composer's deceased parents and partly an anti-militaristic statement. As the only other work in the composer's output to carry the title 'Requiem', its connection with the later *War Requiem* is inescapable. Britten spoke of the *Sinfonia* to the *New York Sun* in a feature published on 27 April 1940: 'I'm making it just as anti-war as possible... I don't believe you can express social or political or economic theories in music, but by coupling new music with well known musical phrases, I think it's possible to get over certain ideas ... all I'm sure of is my own anti-war conviction as I write it.'[44] As with *Ballad of Heroes* one year before, the *Sinfonia* looks directly ahead to the *War Requiem* in numerous respects: from the sombre, deep ostinati of the 'Lacrimosa', through the savage scherzo ('Dies irae') to the beatific diatonic release of the concluding 'Requiem aeternam', the emotional and gestural content is directly comparable to the later work. Especially notable is the 'Dies irae', where the 'dance of death' forms part of a long tradition in Britten's works from as early as *Our Hunting Fathers* ('Hawking') and *Ballad of Heroes* to the culminating cynicism of the brittle setting of 'The Next War' in the 'Dies irae' of the *War Requiem*.

It was only in the early months of 1942 that Britten appears to have begun to think specifically about the possibility of returning to England in order to register officially as a conscientious objector, thereby publicly declaring his pacifism and at the same time providing a tangible artistic and community service to his home country. Press comment during Britten's absence had not been entirely favourable, with Ernest Newman's enthusiastic review of his Violin Concerto in the *Sunday Times* eliciting a barbed response from George Baker of the Royal Philharmonic Society:

In your last issue, Mr Ernest Newman, under the heading 'Thoroughbreds', said he had 'been fighting single-handed the "battle of Britten"'.

There are a number of musicians in this country who are well content to let Mr Newman have this dubious honour. The young gentleman on whose behalf he fights, Mr Benjamin Britten, was born in 1913. He is in America. He may have had perfectly good reasons for going there, and may decide to return to his native land some time or other. In the meantime I would like to remind Mr Newman that most of our musical 'thoroughbreds' are stabled in or near London and are directing all their endeavours towards winning the City and Suburban and the Victory Stakes, two classic events that form part of a programme called the Battle of Britain; a programme in which Mr Britten has no part.[45]

Britten's decision to return home and face a tribunal constituted something of a risk, as it was by no means guaranteed that exemption from military service would be granted. Michael Tippett, for example, appeared before a

Tribunal for the Registration of Conscientious Objectors in February 1942 and was ordered to work full-time as an Air-Raid Precautions warden, fireman or agricultural worker: he declined, and accordingly served three months in Wormwood Scrubs in 1943 (during which sentence Britten visited the prison to give a recital as part of his own 'official' wartime duties).

Britten expressed something of his fear that the outcome of the tribunal hearing might not be in his favour in a letter to Isherwood written on 10 March 1942, one month before he returned home:

Well, things are coming to a head at last, thank God – and there is something tangible to face, instead of Consul and Draft-boards & Exit permits. We have a boat, leaving sometime next Monday. The Brit. Consul is gloomy about the sailing, ie. that there hasn't been a more unpleasant time – but, honestly I don't worry about it now. I am, and have been in an acute work crisis these last 6 months, and I truly believe that if I am intended to do something worth while I'll get thro', and if not – well, it's a painless way out. . .

I'm not really happy about the other side. It'll be lovely to see my family, & Wulff [Scherchen, son of the conductor Hermann Scherchen], and all again; but I am more & more (especially after reading Morgan's Dickinson) convinced that I cannot kill, so it'll be a tribunal, & I am scared stiff of judges & all that. But, pray for me, my dear. . .

Britten arrived back in the United Kingdom on 17 April 1942, and enlisted the aid of Canon Stuart Morris as a supporting character-witness for his impending appearance before a Local Tribunal in London on 28 May. Morris was Liaison Officer to the Central Board of Conscientious Objectors and was General Secretary of the Peace Pledge Union – for whom Britten had composed his *Pacifist March* five years previously – from 1939 to 1943 and subsequently from 1946 to 1964. (Britten was himself a sponsor of the PPU from the end of the war until his death, and in 1947 composed *Canticle I* in memory of the Revd Dick Sheppard, Vicar of St Martin-in-the-Fields, who had been a founder member of the Union in 1934.) The full text of Britten's statement to the Tribunal, dated 4 May, ran as follows:

Since I believe that there is in every man the spirit of God, I cannot destroy, and feel it my duty to avoid helping to destroy as far as I am able, human life, however strongly I may disapprove of the individual's actions or thoughts. The whole of my life has been devoted to acts of creation (being by profession a composer) and I cannot take part in acts of destruction. Moreover, I feel that the fascist attitude to life can only be overcome by passive resistance. If Hitler were in power here or this country had any similar form of government, I should feel it my duty to obstruct this regime in every non-violent way possible, and by complete non-cooperation. I believe sincerely that I can help my fellow human beings best, by continuing the work I am most qualified to do by the nature of my gifts and training, i.e. the creation or propagation of music. I have possibilities of writing music for M[inistry]. O[f]. I[nformation]. films, and for B.B.C. productions, and am offering my services to the Committee for the Encouragement of Music and Art [CEMA]. I am however prepared, but feel completely unsuited by nature & training, to undertake other constructive civilian work provided that it is not connected with any of the armed forces.

From the Tribunal's subsequent report we learn (intriguingly) that Britten also declared 'I do not believe in the Divinity of Christ, but I think his teaching is sound and his example should be followed.'[46] On 3 June, Britten received the Tribunal's unanimous decision to the effect that he remained liable to be called up for non-combatant military service.

With the support of the BBC's Lawrence Gilliam (who attested to the various projected radio commissions envisaged for the composer) and Frank Bridge's widow Ethel (who provided a testimonial revealing how he had hated the military even as a boy), Britten made a formal appeal against this decree and prepared a further statement for the Appellate Tribunal:

That the Local Tribunal failed to appreciate the religious background of my conscience trying to tie me down too narrowly to a belief in the divinity of Christ. I don't seek as suggested to pick & choose from his teaching, but I regard the whole context of his teaching & example as the standard by which I must judge. It is for this reason that my conscientious objection covers non-combatant as well as combatant service in the army... I realise however that in total war, it is impossible to avoid all participation of an indirect kind but I believe that I must draw the line as far away from direct participation as possible. It is for this reason that I appeal to be left free to follow that line of service to the community which my conscience approves & my training makes possible.

The Tribunal reconsidered Britten's case on 18 August and, reaching a favourable verdict, his certificate of unconditional registration as a conscientious objector with no obligation for non-combatant duties was duly issued on 3 May 1943.[47] His only specific requirement was to give concerts for CEMA, in which capacity his meeting with Tippett in Wormwood Scrubs took place on 11 July. Pears had proved luckier: his full exemption had been granted at his first hearing in September 1942.

As is now well known, the opera *Peter Grimes* (completed in 1945) directly reflected the isolation felt by Britten and Pears as conscientious objectors in its sympathetic portrayal of the fisherman ostracized by his community. In an interview with Murray Schafer, Britten looked back on this difficult period and commented:

A central feeling for us was that of the individual against the crowd, with ironic overtones for our own situation. As conscientious objectors we were out of it. We couldn't say we suffered physically, but naturally we experienced tremendous tension. I think it was partly this feeling which led us to make Grimes a character of vision and conflict, the tortured idealist he is, rather than the villain he was in Crabbe.[48]

As with Owen's wavering views on the moral justification of warfare, so Britten's difficult situation produced a 'tremendous tension' leading to impressive artistic results. Significantly, it was the overtly pacifist Isherwood whom Britten first invited to write the libretto for *Grimes* before going on to approach Montagu Slater, who had felt strongly that Britten ought not to have gone to America in 1939. He was also aided in the closing stages of the opera's composition by his pacifist friend Ronald Duncan, who in 1946 attempted to interest Britten in a post-Hiroshima oratorio to be entitled *Mea Culpa*. In spite of the phenomenally successful première of *Grimes* by Sadler's Wells on 7 June 1945, the production had nearly foundered because of hostility towards Britten, Pears and the opera's producer Eric Crozier: all three were 'conchees' (the term with which Owen would have been familiar was 'shirkers'), and many felt it inappropriate that the end of the war should be celebrated with a work of art created by men who had not directly contributed towards the military victory.

The full horrors of the Nazi regime were graphically brought home to Britten in the summer of 1945 when he visited the notorious concentration camp at Belsen with the violinist Yehudi Menuhin to give a recital to the survivors. This harrowing experience, perhaps reflected in the stark musical idiom of *The Holy Sonnets of John Donne* composed immediately afterwards, must have remained in Britten's mind for the rest of his life; but after 1947 a renewed optimism enters his work which is fully in keeping with the general sense of relief affecting the British public after the cessation of hostilities, and renewed hopes for the future symbolized by the crowning of a youthful monarch in 1953. Two years before the coronation, Britten's naval opera *Billy Budd* (set in the Napoleonic wars) might have provided a vehicle for a veiled pacifist message; but any interpretation attempting to equate the mutinous sentiments of the sailors with pacifist symbolism is doomed to failure once it has been noted that their dissatisfaction is intensified by their inability to vent their frustrations on a passing enemy ship.

Britten first revealed his interest in the poetry of Wilfred Owen by choosing 'Strange Meeting' and 'The Kind Ghosts' as part of his celebrity poetry selection for a BBC radio programme in 1958 (see also pp. 28 and 103–4). In the same year, he set 'The Kind Ghosts' to music as one of the numbers in his orchestral song-cycle *Nocturne*. Owen's poem is not explicitly concerned with war or pacifism, but the poet thought highly enough of it to have included the text in his projected collection 'Disabled & Other Poems' at Scarborough in 1918. As it was for this collection that Owen wrote his famous poetic manifesto (quoted in full on p. 10 above), a direct connection between the poem's haunting imagery and the bloodshed of war is plausible enough:

> She sleeps on soft, last breaths; but no ghost looms
> Out of the stillness of her palace wall,
> Her wall of boys on boys and dooms on dooms.
>
> She dreams of golden gardens and sweet glooms,
> Not marvelling why her roses never fall
> Nor what red mouths were torn to make their blooms.
>
> The shades keep down which well might roam her hall.
> Quiet their blood lies in her crimson rooms
> And she is not afraid of their footfall.
>
> They move not from her tapestries, their pall,
> Nor pace her terraces, their hecatombs,
> Lest aught she be disturbed, or grieved at all.

The gory imagery of line 6 reappears in others of Owen's more explicit war poems, most notably in the opening lines of 'Greater Love':

> Red lips are not so red
> As the stained stones kissed by the English dead.

With imagery such as this fresh in his mind, it is not surprising to find Britten selecting Owen's war poems for inclusion in the *War Requiem* two years later.

The *War Requiem* was not to be Britten's final pacifist statement. The compassionate theme of *Cantata Misericordium* in 1963 functioned almost as an epilogue to the larger work, and the composer's views were to remain committed. In 1967, Britten and Pears abruptly left a dinner party when Hans Keller challenged the relevance of their pacifist beliefs to the then current Arab–Israeli war. As Colin Matthews recalled, 'it was an argument about pacifism, for which Ben couldn't provide an intellectual justification, and of course against somebody like Keller he didn't have a chance'.[49] In 1970 Britten returned to a pacifist theme in the television opera *Owen*

Wingrave, his decision to devote this rare opportunity to reach a mass audience to an explicitly anti-war topic clearly reflecting the undiminished strength of his feelings on the subject over the previous decade. In recent years *Wingrave* has come to enjoy a significantly warmer response on the part of critics and audiences alike than at the time of its original broadcast, when it failed to capture the popular imagination as had the *War Requiem* so spectacularly before it; one critic (himself an admirer of the earlier score) went so far as to dismiss the new opera as 'blatant propaganda'.[50]

Unlike Owen and Sassoon, Britten saw no need to 'get some reputation of gallantry' in order for his compassion for his fellow man to acquire public credibility; yet his pacifism was a consistent lifelong commitment, and the sincerity and intensity of its expression in the *War Requiem* ('the one musical masterwork we possess with overt pacifist meanings', as Tippett hailed it[51]) can never be in doubt.

2

The War Requiem *in progress*

PHILIP REED

From the early 1940s Britten had wanted to compose a significant, large-scale choral work that could take its place among the monuments of the English choral tradition. With W. H. Auden he planned a Christmas oratorio (Auden's *For the Time Being*), begun in 1942 in the United States and continued intermittently until 1946 when the scheme was finally abandoned owing to Auden's singular failure to prune the text to a length reasonable for musical setting; in 1945, with Ronald Duncan (librettist of *The Rape of Lucretia*), Britten considered an oratorio entitled *Mea Culpa* designed as a response to the dropping of the atomic bombs on Japan; three years later, following the assassination of Mahatma Gandhi in 1948, Britten's unreserved admiration for the Indian leader, founded on a shared belief in the pacifist cause – and thereby making a more direct link with the *War Requiem* than any other of these unfulfilled projects – caused him to ponder on the possibility of a requiem in his honour; finally, in the mid-1950s, Britten and Duncan entertained a collaboration on another oratorio, this time centred on the life of St Peter and intended for York Minster. While none of the foregoing was ever composed, one might consider that the *Spring Symphony* (1948) fulfilled, at least in part, Britten's need: scored for three soloists, mixed chorus with the addition of a boys' choir (as in the *War Requiem*), and large orchestra, and using a quintessentially Brittenesque anthology of English lyrical verse, the *Spring Symphony* has many of the hallmarks that bring it within the choral tradition Britten wished to satisfy; yet its symphonic shape (a Mahlerian inspiration) and non-religious text in a non-universal language place it to one side of the tradition. When the invitation from the Coventry Festival was made, Britten was ready and waiting to write the kind of work he had long postponed: a setting of the Requiem Mass.

Commission

During the Battle of Britain Coventry had been targeted by the Luftwaffe for concentrated mass-bombing. The city's ancient cathedral was virtually destroyed and, after the war, a decision was made to rebuild the cathedral to a new design. An open competition was held for which the winner, Basil Spence, submitted an imaginative design for a building using modern materials which would be sited adjacent to the shell of the former cathedral. The spirit of the enterprise was one of reconciliation after conflict, reflected in the new cathedral's Chapel of Unity and in allowing the ruins of the former cathedral to remain as a stark reminder of the conflict. Spence wanted his building to be a showcase for the arts and crafts; his structure was enhanced by notable exponents of the arts: for example, Graham Sutherland was commissioned to design an imposing woven tapestry of Christ in Majesty to hang behind the high altar; John Piper (with Patrick Reytiens) executed the vast Baptistry window; and Sir Jacob Epstein created the sculpture of St Michael defeating the Devil positioned on the wall outside the cathedral's main entrance.[1] To celebrate the cathedral's consecration in May 1962, a showcase arts festival was planned by the local authority in association with the Arts Council. In keeping with the ideals behind the building itself, the Coventry Cathedral Festival was from the outset intended as an international as well as a national celebration.

It was against this background that Britten was first approached by John Lowe, a friend of the composer's who was serving on the Festival's Arts Committee, on 7 October 1958. The Committee was interested in commissioning a choral and orchestral work from Britten: 'The new work they seek could be full length or a substantial 30/40 minutes one: its libretto could be sacred or secular... The Committee will be very pleased if this great occasion could help bring forth an important new work from you ... they will be v. pleased if you would conduct it.' Britten responded by return of post:

Would you please tell the Arts Committee at Coventry how touched I was by their kind invitation to write something for the consecration of the new Cathedral in 1962. I should very much like to undertake this – one of the reasons, I must confess, being the, for once, reasonable date attached. Seriously, I should be very honoured to be connected with such a significant and moving occasion, and shall do my best to turn out something worthy of it.

By early December the Coventry authorities were aware that Britten was considering a large-scale choral and orchestral work of a religious nature designed as a full evening, and arrangements were set in hand for the formal commission to be made. It was not, however, until the summer of the following year that S. H. Newsome (representing the Coventry Cathedral Festival) began to formalize arrangements with the composer via his publishers Boosey & Hawkes. It is clear from correspondence between Ernst Roth (of Boosey & Hawkes) and Newsome that the latter was under the mistaken impression that Britten required little or no remuneration for the piece as he had so enthusiastically welcomed the idea of writing a work for Coventry. The composer wrote to Roth on 11 August to make his position quite clear:

My feeling is that to commission a work of this size is a serious matter, and they must be prepared to pay for it just as they have to pay the workmen to build the Cathedral, and will have to pay the Covent Garden Opera, etc. etc. Of course when they suggested the idea to me I was interested, and I am keen on writing the Requiem Mass, but if they do not pay (and I feel it should be a reasonable commission such as you discussed with John Denison, or nothing) they must take their chance as to whether the work will be ready in time or not.

Roth was at pains to point out to Newsome how much work was involved and that the composer had already refused three other commissions and, moreover, postponed still further one project of his own (*Curlew River*), in favour of Coventry. In early September, after Britten and Peter Pears had visited the cathedral, the Coventry Festival made a specific offer of £1,000 as a commissioning fee which they hoped would include the necessary performing fees also; as it was neither Britten nor his publishers, but the Performing Right Society which set and regulated such fees, the Festival Committee was forced to accept the figure as a straight commission. Newsome confirmed the agreement reached between the composer and the Festival Committee in a letter dated 25 November 1960: none of the specific details of the work are mentioned in the agreement, only that it would occupy a whole evening's programme; no completion date is specified, only that the new work would be finished 'in good time' for performance at the Festival; the fee was to be divided into two equal payments, one on completion of the piece, the other on the day of the first performance; and the Festival claimed the right to one further performance as well as to the première and asked that no other performances of the work could be given elsewhere until after 30 June 1962.

In the mean time John Lowe, now promoted to Director of the Festival, was preparing a press release about the event and sought the composer's comments on a paragraph he had drafted about the new work from information gleaned from Britten himself. It is an important document in the chronology of the *War Requiem* as it shows Britten's earliest and most general thoughts about the piece:

His new composition will be a full length Requiem for four soloists, choir and orchestra, in which the sections of the traditional Requiem will be interspersed with poems by Wilfred Owen. A Festival Choir, representing the Diocese, is in process of formation, for this and other choral works during the Festival, and it will be trained by Meredith Davies.

Britten responded later that month to Lowe's draft. He was cautious about mentioning the use of Owen's poetry as no arrangements had yet been formalized with Owen's estate or his publishers:

I would much rather in the press release that there is no mention of the Wilfred Owen poems. If you could just say that the new composition will be a Requiem Mass for soloists, choir and orchestra. Most likely the work will be as I described it to you earlier, but I hate to be committed to these things until a later stage in the writing of the work.

It was not until 1961 that formal arrangements with Owen's publishers, Chatto & Windus, were settled.

Composition

It is not known for certain when Britten began work on the composition draft of the *War Requiem* (see pp. 24–5), although if he followed his usual practice then there would have been considerable planning of the broad structural shape of the piece before any of the musical detail was committed to manuscript paper. For the first two months of 1961 Britten was compelled to remain for the most part at home in Aldeburgh, 'quietly (??) working' as he told William Plomer; during this period he completed the Cello Sonata for Rostropovich begun in December of the previous year, and made a setting of the *Jubilate Deo* at the request of the Duke of Edinburgh. But after a Dutch and German tour with Pears in April, and before the considerable demands of the Aldeburgh Festival in early July took hold, Britten cleared his desk to begin the difficult task of composing the *War Requiem*.

Unlike many of Britten's large-scale compositions, the *War Requiem* makes very few appearances in the composer's personal correspondence, perhaps because Britten thought of it as a rather private, personal work in spite of its very obvious public statement of the pacifist position. He disclosed to

Anthony Gishford (of Boosey & Hawkes) on 24 April: 'I am going into Purdah now, trying hard to get on with the new masterpiece for Coventry, & apart from brief dashes for recordings won't be coming to London.' Later in the same letter he suggests that early progress on the *War Requiem* was not fluent. In May he divulged further details of the work's requirements to John Lowe in a letter (12 May 1961) which shows already how important the spatial organization of the work was:

... I am all in favour of as big a chorus as is possible, without passengers... The orchestra will be big, however, as I am planning for certainly triple woodwind and a nice assortment of brass for the 'Tuba Mirum' (possibly as many as fourteen). Then there is the chamber orchestra to make room for, and I think the best position would be immediately in front of the conductor with the two male soloists.[2] The boys, however, I would like to have placed at a distance; they perform throughout only with the organ, so it would be good if they were near the organ console. I realise there is no gallery in Coventry, but I am sure some remote position can be found for them.

By August Britten was able to predict that the 'preliminary work', i.e. the composition draft and the vocal and chorus scores, for the 'Owen–Mass' would be finished by Christmas (letter to William Plomer, 11 August 1961); in a letter to Basil Coleman (29 October 1961), Britten wrote: 'I go on working at the Coventry piece. Sometimes it seems the best ever, more often the worst – but it is always so with me.' Earlier that month Britten appears to have taken a decision about the work's title (to date it had simply been referred to as the 'Requiem Mass'), for he expressly asked for it to be known as the 'War Requiem' in the announcement in the Festival brochure.

Exceptionally for Britten, but as was absolutely essential if the work was ever to be managed by the large body of amateur singers involved, sections of the *War Requiem* vocal score, prepared for Boosey & Hawkes by Imogen Holst (Britten's amanuensis), were made available to the performers before the work was completed. The vocal/chorus score was produced in batches as Britten finished each section of the work. Although full details of the history of this document can no longer be reconstructed with absolute precision, the chronology of the vocal score is a useful indication of Britten's compositional progress. It would seem that the first two sections, the 'Requiem aeternam' and 'Dies irae', were available at the earliest rehearsals held in September 1961 – Britten probably composed these movements in the period of activity preceding the Aldeburgh Festival; the 'Offertorium' may have reached Coventry in time for a rehearsal in early December, and in the same month, while Britten worked on the final section, the 'Libera me', he was asking Boosey & Hawkes for news of the proofs of the 'Sanctus' and 'Agnus Dei'.

A few days before Christmas, on 20 December, Britten completed the composition draft. The manuscript full score (see p. 46 below) was completed during a working holiday in Greece the following month: Britten remarked to Reg Close (the British Council Representative in Greece), in a letter written after his return (28 February 1962), 'people are amazed that I managed to finish my big score and yet also see so much of the wonderful country'.

One issue of some interest that arose during the composition of the *War Requiem* was Britten's growing fascination with Wilfred Owen the man, as opposed to Owen the poet. During the 1961 Aldeburgh Festival Britten mentioned his interest in Owen's biography to Plomer who promised to locate Owen's surviving brother, Harold, then at work on his three-volume life of Wilfred, and to find a photograph of the poet for the composer. For a photograph, Plomer directed Britten to two editions of the poems: that edited by Edmund Blunden (1931), and an earlier one edited by Siegfried Sassoon (1920) (see p. 28 below). Plomer also suggested that a meeting between Harold Owen and the composer might be beneficial, a proposition that Britten resisted; as he told Plomer (16 July 1961): 'I'm not sure about visiting the brother – I am so involved with the work that the chance may not present itself, & also I don't want to be disturbed, maybe, in that direction... Perhaps later, when the work is nearer completion.'

The quest for photographs of Owen continued. During the summer of 1961 Christopher Isherwood, an old friend and collaborator from the 1930s, attempted to get in touch with Britten during one of his infrequent visits to England (Isherwood had lived on the West Coast of the United States since the 1940s). Although it seems improbable that they were reunited – Britten's composing and concert schedule left little spare time to him – Isherwood was aware of Britten's current interest in Owen; on his return to California he sent the composer a copy of an unidentified Sitwell volume in which appeared a photograph of Owen. Britten thanked Isherwood on 11 September: 'I am delighted to have it – I am so involved with him at the moment, & I wanted to see what he looked like: I might have guessed, it's just what I expected really.'[3]

Arrangements for the first performance

Throughout the period of composition plans were being laid for the first performance of the *War Requiem*, destined for 30 May 1962 (broadcast live on the BBC Third Programme) with a second performance in the cathedral on 1 June. As early as 1 February 1961, when Britten was still planning the work, he was to ask John Lowe to engage the Melos Ensemble as the chamber orchestra for the crucial Owen settings even though he had yet to finalize arrangements in respect of the soloists required. Lowe had already engaged the City of Birmingham Symphony Orchestra as the main orchestra. On 9 February Britten wrote again to Lowe about the artists he needed for the work:

As I plan the work it seems more and more clear to me that we need a really first-class, intelligent baritone, to handle the Owen poems along with Peter [Pears]. I have thought a great deal, and discussed the matter with Peter, and we feel the ideal person musically, and also under the circumstances for this particular occasion, would be [Dietrich] Fischer-Dieskau... I expect also to need a strong soprano for the Mass section, but this will not be so difficult to find, and we can discuss it at a later stage in the writing of the work. Conductor?

Britten wrote to Fischer-Dieskau later that month, describing the general nature and purpose of the *War Requiem* but in particular the role of the Owen settings: 'These magnificent poems, full of the hate of destruction, are a kind of commentary on the Mass... They will need singing with the utmost beauty, intensity and sincerity.' Fischer-Dieskau, with whom Pears had occasionally sung, happily agreed to participate, although at one stage, when his involvement was in doubt, Britten's second choice, Hermann Prey – another *German* baritone – was tentatively approached.

Although Lowe had already placed before Britten two distinguished candidates for the soprano part – Elisabeth Schwarzkopf and Amy Shuard – Britten was far more interested in the Russian soprano Galina Vishnevskaya, wife of his newly made friend, the cellist Mstislav Rostropovich. Although Britten knew something of Vishnevskaya's art from recordings, he wisely mistrusted these as a basis on which to write for her; when she accompanied her husband to the 1961 Aldeburgh Festival he had the opportunity to sample the remarkable passion of her singing in a recital she and Rostropovich gave. Her impact on Britten was immediate and he could remain equivocal no longer. Vishnevskaya recalls that Britten approached her after the concert and 'said he was particularly glad he had heard me right at that moment because he had begun to write his *War Requiem* and now wanted to write in a part for me ... his composition, which was a call for peace, would bring together representatives of the three nations that had suffered most during the war: an Englishman, Peter Pears; a German, Fischer-Dieskau;

and a Russian, myself'.[4] Britten made a formal request for her participation in a letter to the formidable Soviet Minister of Culture, Madame Ekaterina Furtseva, on 9 August 1961, in which he was at pains to show that his intentions in engaging an international cast of soloists had been 'to emphasize the universal desire for peace'. In December Lowe received a letter from the Director of GosConcert refusing, without any explanation, Vishnevskaya's participation; Lowe subsequently told Britten (11 December) that their request had been carefully considered but that the refusal was not connected to the work's obvious relationship to the Church, as he and Britten had first believed, but to the Anglo–German–Russian alliance of soloists. Britten made a further plea, this time to Vladimir Stepanov (Ministry of Culture), but to no avail. Up to the last few days before the première, Vishnevskaya hoped that the Soviet authorities would change their minds, amazed that they could refuse such a request from a distinguished foreigner; but shortly before the first performance, after singing *Aida* at Covent Garden, she was summoned back to Moscow, according to Vishnevskaya to appear in a television show and powerless to refuse.[5] Heather Harper sang the soprano part at extremely short notice at the first performance instead.

The final artistic question to be resolved was that of the conductor at the première. Although Lowe and the Festival Committee very much hoped that Britten himself would appear in this role, the composer warned them at the outset that he was never truly comfortable directing large forces. Meredith Davies, who was working at this period with the English Opera Group, was responsible for training the large amateur chorus, a representative body of singers drawn from a selection of smaller choruses in the Midlands region, and for a time it seemed likely that he might undertake the second performance while Britten would have sole responsibility for the première. (It is this arrangement which is shown in the Coventry Festival's programme book.) Britten's reluctance to conduct caused Lowe to suggest other names, and Solti and Giulini were both put forward as possible candidates in place of, or alongside, the composer. In the event, Britten suggested the most practical solution: Davies should direct the main orchestra and choir (the latter would be familiar with his style and manner from their long months of rehearsals together), and he would take responsibility for the tenor and baritone soloists and the chamber orchestra, with whom he would feel most comfortable. This proved to be a pattern of performance that Britten adopted whenever he was involved in performances of the work, for example, with Giulini at Edinburgh in 1968;[6] it was only for his 1963 Decca recording of the *War Requiem* (see pp. 80–1) and at a single Festival Hall performance later that same year that he directed all the forces.

Sources

The Owen texts

The contents of Britten's library suggest that he probably owned only one edition of Owen's poems while he was planning the *War Requiem*: a 1955 impression of Edmund Blunden's 1931 edition published by Chatto & Windus. However, Britten may also have had access to Owen's *Poems*, with an Introduction by Siegfried Sassoon, published by Chatto & Windus in 1920. Sassoon, assisted by Edith Sitwell, was the first to thread his way through the maze of Owen's manuscripts, from which he selected twenty-three poems and fragments, adding a twenty-fourth for the 1921 reissue. The edition includes a frontispiece portrait of Owen in uniform. Britten owned two copies of the first edition, one of which was certainly given to him after the *War Requiem* had been performed; it is not known when he acquired the other copy. Britten has not marked either copy and they evidently played no direct role in the work's composition.

The Blunden edition – *The poems of Wilfred Owen*, edited with a Memoir and notes by Edmund Blunden – was Britten's principal source for all the Owen texts used in the *War Requiem* and is heavily marked with the composer's characteristic pencil annotations. Britten most likely purchased it before 1960 (the date of the subsequent reprint of the edition) and may have used it as the source of the text for the setting he made of Owen's 'The Kind Ghosts' in his *Nocturne*, Op. 60, in 1958, the same year he included 'Strange Meeting', subsequently to form the final Owen setting in the *War Requiem*, in a selection of verse he made for a BBC radio programme.[7]

Britten marked his selection of poems with a simple pencil 'X'; and all of them found their way into the piece with the exception of 'Arms and the Boy', the quasi-erotic imagery of which may have precluded its inclusion (see below, p. 36). Three poems – 'Sonnet (On Seeing a Piece of Our Artillery Brought into Action)', 'Voices', and 'Strange Meeting' – have further annotations which show the cuts Britten found necessary for musical setting. 'Sonnet' ('Be slowly lifted up, thou long black arm') is reduced to a mere six lines by Britten who, in placing the poem immediately before the reprise of the 'Dies irae', makes an ironic juxtaposition: the destructive force of the 'long black arm' of the artillery and the catastrophic Day of Judgement are one and the same. The fragmentary 'Voices' ('Bugles sang, saddening the evening air') is, according to Jon Stallworthy, possibly a preliminary draft for 'Anthem for Doomed Youth', the first of Britten's Owen settings in the *War Requiem*.[8] If this relationship were not actually known to the composer, it may have at least been sensed by him and explicate his placing of the two poems in relative proximity. Once again, the choice of the Owen text in relation to the liturgy – in this case following the fanfare-obsessed 'Dies irae' – shows Britten's skill in setting up an ironic conflict of verbal and musical messages.

'Strange Meeting' has numerous pencil annotations and erasure markings, far exceeding any other poem in the volume, which show the extent to which Britten was at pains to refashion this text to his own purposes (see Plate 1). The number of erasure markings and the pencil's still-visible impression on the page suggest that the composer found some difficulty in finding a satisfactory reshaping of this long poem, and we note his incorporation of alternative (and discarded) readings taken from Blunden's editorial notes. Britten's omission of four lines (lines 9–12) –

> And by his smile, I knew that sullen hall,
> By his dead smile I knew we stood in Hell.
> With a thousand pains that vision's face was grained;
> Yet no blood reached there from the upper ground.

– is striking in the light of his predisposition throughout the piece towards ironic juxtaposition of Owen's poetry and the timeless words of the Latin ritual. This confrontation of private and public worlds and morals, themselves an important theme in Britten's art from the 1930s onwards, might have played its strongest hand had he faced up to the power of these words and chosen to set, rather than omit, them (see pp. 74–5). The Hell of Owen's encounter in death between soldiers from opposing sides of the conflict, in contrast to the vision of Paradise offered by the liturgy, might have proved the ultimate unsettling, discomforting irony.

Britten makes two further striking marginalia in the volume. In Edmund Blunden's 1931 prefatory Memoir, Britten makes a single vertical stroke in the margin opposite a passage from one of Owen's letters from the hospital on the Somme, a letter in which the subject of pacifism is raised, as well as the dubious nature of conventional religious dogma, two ideas which Britten seeks to confront us with in the *War Requiem*:

Already I have comprehended a light which never will filter into the dogma of any national church: namely, that one of Christ's essential commands was: Passivity at any

STRANGE MEETING

It seemed that out of battle I escaped
Down some profound dull tunnel, long since scooped
Through granites which titanic wars had groined.
Yet also there encumbered sleepers groaned,
Too fast in thought or death to be bestirred.
Then, as I probed them, one sprang up, and stared
With piteous recognition in fixed eyes,
Lifting distressful hands as if to bless.
And by his smile, I knew that sullen hall,
By his dead smile I knew we stood in Hell.
With a thousand pains that vision's face was grained;
Yet no blood reached there from the upper ground
And no guns thumped, or down the flues made moan.
"Strange friend," I said, "here is no cause to mourn."
"None," said the other, "save the undone years,
The hopelessness. Whatever hope is yours,
Was my life also; I went hunting wild
After the wildest beauty in the world,
Which lies not calm in eyes, or braided hair,
But mocks the steady running of the hour,
And if it grieves, grieves richlier than here.
For by my glee might many men have laughed,
And of my weeping something had been left,
Which must die now. I mean the truth untold,
The pity of war, the pity war distilled.
Now men will go content with what we spoiled,
Or, discontent, boil bloody, and be spilled.
They will be swift with swiftness of the tigress,
None will break ranks, though nations trek from progress.
Courage was mine, and I had mystery,
Wisdom was mine, and I had mastery;
To miss the march of this retreating world

Miss we

Into vain citadels that are not walled.
Then, when much blood had clogged their chariot-wheels
I would go up and wash them from sweet wells,
~~Even with truths that lie too deep for taint.~~
~~I would have poured my spirit without stint~~
~~But not through wounds; not on the cess of war.~~
~~Foreheads of men have bled where no wounds were.~~
I am the enemy you killed, my friend.
I knew you in this dark; for so you frowned
Yesterday through me as you jabbed and killed.
I parried; but my hands were loath and cold.
Let us sleep now. . . .".

Even from wells we sunk too deep for war,
Even the sweetest well that ever were

Plate 1   Owen's 'Strange Meeting', with Britten's pencil annotations.

price! Suffer dishonour and disgrace, but never resort to arms. Be bullied, be outraged, be killed; but do not kill. It may be chimerical and an ignominious principle, but there it is. It can only be ignored; and I think pulpit professionals are ignoring it very skilfully and successfully indeed... And am I not myself a conscientious objector with a very seared conscience? ... Christ is literally in 'no man's land'. There men often hear His voice: Greater love hath no man than this, that a man lay down his life for a friend. Is it spoken in English only and in French? I do not believe so. Thus you see how pure Christianity will not fit in with pure patriotism.[9]

Although Britten would not have agreed with Owen's estimation of pacifism as both 'chimerical' and 'ignominious', taken as a whole the passage must have set up a profound resonance with his own long-held pacific beliefs.

The other passage marked for special note comes from the Appendix to the volume, a brief reminiscence of Owen in 1917 by Frank Nicholson, Librarian of Edinburgh University, who became acquainted with Owen when he was invalided at Craiglockhart Hospital. It is related to the first marked passage and, in essence, lies at the very heart of the *War Requiem* as an act of reparation between mankind:

[Owen's] sense of pity, which must have been strong in him by nature and had been intensified by his experiences, enabled him to regard Germany as a fellow-sufferer with the rest and made him wish, I think, to prepare himself for any future opportunities of holding intercourse with the Germans *or any other enemy* (my italics).[10]

Although it was not first published until over a year after the *War Requiem* was premièred, we note that Britten purchased, at the earliest opportunity, C. Day Lewis's edition of *The collected poems of Wilfred Owen*.

Britten's notebook

As was his habitual practice, Britten wrote out the entire libretto of the *War Requiem* – the Owen poems (incorporating the emendations already discussed) and the words from the *Missa pro defunctis* (with his own English translation when required) – in one of his old school exercise books dating from 1928. The notebook has been used in two directions: from the front, as Britten the schoolboy's German notebook; and from the back and inverted, as a notebook in which Britten the mature composer could experiment with and assemble possible texts for musical setting. The notebook comprises seventy-three folios bound in red boards measuring 22.8 x 17.7 cm.

(*GB–ALb*: 1–9300837), and covers works from 1958 to 1963. Its contents may be summarized:

[front board]	'BB / <u>TEXTS</u>'
[verso of front board]	'Possible sequence' of poems for *Nocturne*, Op. 60; among Britten's list is Owen's 'The Kind Ghosts'
fol. [1ʳ–12ʳ]	Texts for *Nocturne* (called 'Dreams'), including some poems not set
fol. [12ᵛ–16ʳ]	Text for *Cantata Academica*, Op. 62
fol. [17ʳ–29ʳ]	Draft scenarios for *A Midsummer Night's Dream*, Op. 64
fol. [30ʳ–31ʳ]	Notes concerning Britten's Purcell realizations
fol. [31ᵛ–40ʳ]	Text of *War Requiem*, Op. 66
fol. [40ᵛ–44ʳ]	Text of *The Bitter Withy*, of which Britten made a setting (unfinished) for tenor, boys' choir and piano
fol. [44ᵛ–46ʳ]	First text of *Cantata Misericordium* (Latin, with English translation)
fol. [47ʳ–48ᵛ]	'Possible early horrors': a list of songs from Britten's juvenilia which he thought might be worthy of revival
fol. [49ʳ–54ʳ]	Text (revised) of *Cantata Misericordium*
fol. [54ᵛ–73ᵛ]	The schoolboy Britten's German notebook, but inverted and therefore in reverse order

For the text of the *War Requiem* Britten employed double-page spreads to accommodate his layout: the words of the Requiem Mass are written in pencil on the far left, with his own translation (as required) occupying the central position; the Owen poems are placed on the far right with brackets and arrows to indicate their precise location in the sequence of the liturgy. The Owen texts are written in ink or ballpoint which may suggest that they were inscribed at a different time (perhaps later?) than the text of the Requiem Mass. For the Owen texts Britten indicates in pencil (again, perhaps an indication of decisions made on a different occasion) which voice (tenor, baritone, or both) is assigned to which poem.

The Latin text has been cut in a number of places – for instance, in the 'Dies irae' at the famous words beginning 'Lux aeterna luceat eis' – and a deleted sequence of roman numerals shows that at one stage Britten considered subdividing the work into a far greater number of sections than the six main movements to be found in the ultimate arrangement. Below the words of the 'In paradisum' Britten has notated the plainsong which is

IV

Sanctus, sanctus, sanctus, Dominus Deus, Sabaoth
Pleni sunt caeli et terra gloria tua Hosanna
in excelsis.
Benedictus qui venit in nomine Domini. Hosanna
i excelsis

V

? nobis pacem

Agnus Dei, qui tollis peccata mundi : dona eis requiem

Agnus Dei, qui tollis peccata mundi dona eis
requiem sempiternam.

lux aeterna luceat eis
Domine, Cum sanctis tuis i
aeternam, quia pius es.
Requiem aeternam dona eis
Domine Cum Sanctis etc

72.

34

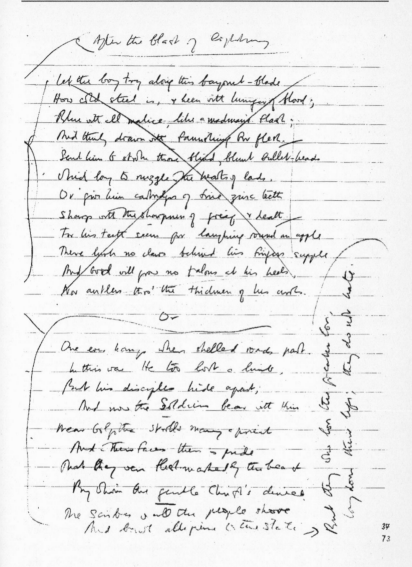

35

incorporated into the *War Requiem*'s final pages (cf. the boys' choir and organ at Fig. 128). The Owen texts have been copied from the Blunden edition *without* the cuts subsequently imposed by the composer: these omissions were evidently a direct result of the poems' location within the overall liturgical framework.

Occasionally Britten's placing of a poem deviates from the published score – for example, 'Be slowly lifted up, thou long black arm' is located before the lines 'Oro supplex et acclinis, / Cor contritum quasi cinis: / Gere curam mei finis', not after them – but otherwise in this respect the draft libretto corresponds for the most part to the published arrangement. Only in one instance is there any evidence of Britten choosing a poem which was rejected and subsequently replaced by another. In the 'Agnus Dei', a key moment in the work where the worldly and spiritual are drawn together, Britten originally wanted to use Owen's 'Arms and the Boy' (see above, p. 28), a poem he rejected in favour of 'At a Calvary near the Ancre' ('One ever hangs where shelled roads part') (see Plate 2). The same pages on which the substitution was made carry further evidence of Pears's involvement in the shaping of the text: he adds (in pencil) '? nobis pacem' above the words from the Requiem Mass 'dona eis requiem'. It would appear that the words 'Dona nobis pacem' – taken from the Ordinary of the Mass, *not* from the Requiem Mass itself – which are so movingly located at the close of Owen's 'One ever hangs' were in fact an inspired suggestion of Pears's.[11]

Composition draft

The composition draft of the *War Requiem* (*GB–Lbl* Add. MS No. 60609) comprises 102 folios of 24-stave manuscript paper, measuring 36.5 x 27 cm., bound in blue boards with a leather spine and corners. It is dated on the final page: 'Aldeburgh Dec. 20th 1961'.

A few general words on the nature of Britten's draft and its related discarded leaves are necessary, although it is impossible in the context of the present discussion to explore these documents in exhaustive detail. The pattern of Britten's working methods hardly ever varied and the disciplined routine adopted in early adulthood was maintained, with only very few exceptions, with unfailing regularity. Britten's business-like timetable for the working day is well attested: two main periods of composition at his desk (not his piano), one in the morning, the other in the late afternoon/early evening, framed a long 'thinking' walk after lunch. He always mistrusted working at night, although scoring might be undertaken then if a deadline were fast approaching. By adhering to this rigorous schedule, Britten was usually able to judge the amount of time needed to complete a major composition with unnerving accuracy.

As with the vast majority of Britten's output, the *War Requiem* took shape on the manuscript paper as a through-composed short score draft written in pencil throughout, with the orchestral texture reduced onto two, three or occasionally four staves and the vocal lines occupying their own staves. At first glance the draft resembles something approaching a vocal score and was certainly used as a guide by Imogen Holst when she prepared the vocal score (under Britten's supervision) for Boosey & Hawkes. The instrumentation is indicated by verbal abbreviations – 'str', 'trbn', 'ww' – at the time of composition, ready for instant retrieval when the moment came for the full score to be made. This simple technique was effective in allowing Britten to press on to the end of a work before making the full score, safe in the knowledge that the piece was in effect written; in the case of complex works, such as the *War Requiem*, it also allowed an assistant to follow behind the composer using the draft as a basis for the all-important vocal score from which the soloists and chorus would learn their music. Once a new piece was complete in draft form, the business of making the corresponding full score was largely a calligraphic labour; the vast majority of problems had already presented themselves and solutions been found.

Throughout his career Britten preferred to work in pencil when composing because of the freedom it offered for changes of mind; the use of pencil was a significantly liberating factor to the composer's creativity since anything that was committed to paper might be easily rubbed out and rewritten. Almost every leaf of the *War Requiem* draft shows evidence of the use of the eraser, demonstrating unequivocally how closely Britten tested his original ideas. By and large it is not very easy to read the rubbed-out notes, although occasionally one can discern the impression made by Britten's pencil and decipher something valuable.

Two other, related, methods of making changes to a work can be found on any of Britten's composition drafts. Rather than erasing passages, particularly if they were more than a few bars, Britten would cross-through a section which he wished to delete. Occasionally, if the deleted passage amounted to a full page, he might detach it from the bifolium and use the available blank verso elsewhere in the manuscript draft. If more than one page were rejected then Britten would almost always remove the offending passage from the main draft and place the particular folio(s) to one side. These discarded leaves form an important category of substantial earlier versions of the music.

Much of the foregoing holds true for Britten's methods while working on the *War Requiem*, and his work on the draft generated a quantity of discarded leaves. In two places in the work – the settings of Owen's 'Anthem for Doomed Youth' and 'Move him into the sun' – the number of discarded composition-draft pages is, even for Britten, unusually large and varied in scope, suggesting that the composer experienced greater difficulty in defining and refining his ideas than was customary. What is undoubtedly embodied in all the draft pages for the *War Requiem*, however, bears testimony to just how remarkably successful Britten was at planning out his music in advance of committing the actual notes to the page: in effect, the long, thinking walks were where much of the compositional thought processes sifted through and refined musical ideas. The composition draft and accompanying discarded pages (in the case of the *War Requiem*, the majority of the latter are bound with the main draft) offer, even at best, a relatively and necessarily limited view of the workings of the creative mind; they only represent the tangible by-products of Britten's skilful and inspired art in bridging the differing, often disparate, elements that make up the complex compositional process.

The salient features of the draft may be summarized movement by movement:

I   Requiem aeternam
A discarded version (eighteen bars) of the opening of the work exists (fol. 71^r–71^v), which approximates to the published version as far as seven bars after Fig. 1. Many features of the final version of this memorable passage are present, including the funereal gong strokes, the tolling bells (F sharp–C) and the solemn, almost lumbering, orchestral march, though occasionally the detail of the pitches differs. Unlike the published score, this discarded sketch has uncomplicated homophonic choral entries in octaves (S+T; A+B) intoning the timeless words of comfort. Only at 'dona eis Domine' does Britten introduce overlapping vocal entries, shortly after which the sketch breaks off. This change of approach clearly set off in the composer's mind the possibility of introducing such an effect from the beginning of the movement, a detail which offers far greater atmosphere.[12]

Fol. 72^r comprises what is probably the first notation of the boys' choir's entry at 'Te decet hymnus', a sketch that corresponds to the music between Figs. 3 and 4. It is a true sketch page and never formed part of the main composition-draft sequence. The page contains two versions of the passage in question, the second a development of the first. Neither quite adheres to the vocal line as published, but both are demonstrably close to it. Both sketches incorporate a chordal accompaniment which points the way to the final draft, the second being the nearest. The second version has two sets of accompanying chords, the first of which is deleted. The second (later) sequence also includes a hint of the ostinato pitches (C–F sharp) played by the main orchestra in the final version (see Ex. 2.1). This sketch page also contains an example of what proved to be a familiar Britten habit: the writing down of a full chromatic scale with the pitches crossed through as Britten used up the notes (or the chords they represent). The impersonal quality of the boys' choir is accentuated in 'Te decet' by the use of a sequence of chords each one of which is based on a different pitch. In effect, it is a subtle use of a twelve-note proposition in a wholly – and wholly characteristic – tonal context.

In spite of sketching the boys' first entry, Britten still evidently found dissatisfaction with his earlier thoughts on this passage: fol. 69^r–69^v is a

Ex. 2.1

24-bar deleted section corresponding to five bars after Fig. 3 to seven bars after Fig. 6. This leaf corresponds to fol. 5ʳ–5ᵛ in the main draft, and we note the twelve crossed-through bars on fol. 4ᵛ which represents a still earlier continuation of this material.

Evidence of frequent use of an eraser on the pages containing the first Owen setting ('What passing-bells', for tenor) suggests that Britten experienced some difficulties in drafting this setting. The struggle to find an appropriate expression for Owen's haunting words produced no less than five discarded attempts, not all of which are complete. These rejected versions may be found on fol. 73ʳ–77ᵛ. While a definitive chronological order for these leaves is difficult to establish, they may be summarized as follows:

(1) fol. 73ʳ–73ᵛ: A draft that corresponds to the passage between Fig. 9 to six bars after Fig. 11. The vocal line begins with repeated Cs familiar from the final version but with a changed rhythmic profile. The harp's 'bisbigliando' and the shapes of the woodwind flourishes are present; however, the mocking dotted figure in the strings is missing, with a consequent lack of energy to the setting. The 'anger of the guns' is depicted by side drum only, i.e. without the strings and bass drum which make such a memorable contribution in Britten's final version.

(2) fol. 74ʳ–74ᵛ: A further draft of the same passage which may be an earlier version of fol. 73; the pair of leaves have many ideas in common. The vocal line begins in a similar fashion to the draft notated on fol. 73, but quickly diverges from it. The 'anger of the guns' is here represented by a simple quaver figure on strings; no percussion is indicated.

(3) fol. 75ʳ–75ᵛ: A further draft corresponding to the previous leaves, though it is undoubtedly closer to fol. 73, which may suggest that in fact fol. 74 is the earliest. A version of the repeated string figuration at 'anger of the guns' is present. Fol. 75ᵛ contains sketches for what finally became the string figure at Fig. 9, material that was incorporated onto the version drafted on fol. 77ʳ–77ᵛ. Further sketches for this material were made on fol. 76ʳ.

(4) fol. 76ʳ–76ᵛ: Another attempt at the same passage in which the vocal line is clearly becoming closer to shapes recognizable from the published version. The harp writing diverges from the final version in this draft.

(5) fol. 77ʳ–77ᵛ: An extended draft corresponding to the passage between Figs. 9 and 12. It is more extended and 'finished' than any of the previous attempts, and has most of the features of the final version (fol.

7ʳ–9ᵛ). Unless an intermediate attempt is now missing, this draft must surely have preceded the final version.[13]

The final bars of the opening section, the 'Kyrie eleison' for unaccompanied chorus punctuated by the tolling bells, were reconsidered after an initial draft (now crossed through on the main draft (fol. 9ᵛ)).

II Dies irae

Ex. 2.2 is an exact transcription of a sketch (fol. 70ʳ) of the brass fanfares that open the movement, a sketch which most probably represents the first written form of this seminal material. As Ex. 2.2 shows, Britten made two attempts at the passage; the final version combines elements from both. The return of the fanfares at Fig. 22 (after 'Coget omnes ante thronum') caused Britten a moment's thought as evinced by a rejected draft of this section of the movement (fol. 80ʳ).

One leaf of the baritone's first Owen setting was rewritten (compare fol. 81ʳ–81ᵛ, the discarded draft, with fol. 14ʳ–14ᵛ), although the differences are minimal when compared to the difficulties Britten found with the tenor's

Ex. 2.2

first Owen setting. Elsewhere in the 'Dies irae' there are minimal (and relatively uninteresting) redrafted passages, sometimes of only a few bars' duration: for example, in the soprano's 'Liber scriptus' (her first entry), the chorus entries at 'Quid sum miser tunc dicturus' and in the tenor–baritone parodying duet, 'Out there, we've walked quite friendly up to Death'. A more substantial reconsideration took place at the 'Recordare' where the orchestral introduction (Figs. 39–40) originally included a version of the 'Recordare' theme on brass, thereby making the the theme's relationship to the opening fanfares particularly clear (fol. 82^r–82^v).

The alteration of the 'Lacrimosa' and the tenor's 'Move him into the sun' required some redrafting before Britten was satisfied, in particular the Owen setting of which the many abandoned drafts are comparable to the level of rethinking that took place in the 'Requiem aeternam'. A deleted version of the close of this section exists within the main body of the composition draft in which Britten sets the words of the 'Pie Jesu' not as in the published score – i.e. as a reprise of the cadential figures first heard at the close of the 'Requiem aeternam' – but to the 'Lacrimosa' motif with a homophonic, almost Verdian parlando chanting of the words 'dona eis requiem' on the all-important pitches of C and G flat (=F sharp), which clearly relate the material to the central tritone axis of the work. Part of the original ending to the movement is transcribed as Ex. 2.3.

Ex. 2.3

Among the discarded leaves can be found several attempts at the setting of 'Move him into the sun'; each begins in a similar manner, i.e. with the chorus and solo soprano's 'Judicandus homo reus' (four bars before Fig. 56). The different attempts may be summarized as follows:

(1) fol. 84^r–84^v: Most probably the first attempt. The vocal line and harmonies differ from the published version; in addition to the string tremolando (present in the finished work), Britten included echoes of the tenor line which he subsequently excluded. The draft breaks off around the words 'Always it woke him' (there is no text present in this draft). Ex. 2.4 is a transcription of part of this leaf.

In addition, fol. 84^v includes an attempt at the vocal line alone, which proves closer to the rhythmic profile of the final draft than the draft made on fol. 84^r–84^v.

(2) fol. 85^r–86^v: A substantial draft of the same passage as (1) above, in which the orchestral imitation of the vocal line is present but here more convincingly formed. This draft breaks off three bars after the chorus's interpolation of 'Qua resurget'.

(3) fol. 87^r–88^v: Another substantial attempt at the same passage in which Britten moves closer to his final version (the orchestral imitation is now expunged). This (third) attempt reaches the end of the movement with a first version of the choral 'Pie Jesu ... Amen' echoing the tenor soloist. Britten may have abandoned this idea as it draws together the ritual grief of the Latin text and the song's *real* expression of grief (the soldier of Owen's poem is beyond consolation) in a way that was to be achieved more effectively in the 'Agnus Dei'. Britten's second attempt at the close of the 'Lacrimosa' (fol. 29^v) incorporates the soprano's 'weeping' motif.

III Offertorium

The draft of the compact 'Offertorium' is freer of evidence of the use of the eraser than any of the previous sections of the work. This is, perhaps, to be expected as Britten is reworking previously composed material for a substantial part of the movement (i.e. the incorporation of material from *Canticle II: Abraham and Isaac*). Discarded drafts are extant for the opening of the movement (as far as four bars after Fig. 61), for the baritone's entry ('So Abram rose ...'), and for the boys' 'Hostias'. The latter (fol. 89^r) is a genuine sketch of this material, devoid of its relationship to the Owen setting.

Ex. 2.4

IV Sanctus

A fragmentary sketch of the 'Sanctus' melody on the verso of a discarded cover of the manuscript vocal score of the 'Offertorium' shows Britten carefully testing his material (Ex. 2.5) as he feels his way towards the final version. A pair of discarded drafts of the opening of the movement survive. One, which is a mere five bars long (fol. 90^r), breaks off at the soprano's melisma; the basic material, however, is very similar to the published score. The other rejected draft is in private ownership and comprises a single leaf which takes the movement through to the first bars of the choral 'Pleni sunt coeli' (the leaf is a first draft of fol. 41, the same passage in the main composition draft). The most interesting divergence from the published score concerns the setting of the words 'Pleni sunt coeli et terra gloria tua', which the divided chorus freely chant on approximate pitches; in his first draft Britten specified that the pitches were to be sung in the conventional way. Even in his subsequent draft (fol. 41) it is possible to see that the chorus parts' noteheads have been crudely altered to accommodate this change of mind.

Further unsuccessful drafts from this movement include the transition from the 'Hosanna' to the 'Benedictus' (fol. 91^r–92^v) and the close of the

Ex. 2.5

'Benedictus' leading back into the reprise of the 'Hosanna' (fol. 90^v). In the latter Britten included further material for the soprano soloist.

V Agnus Dei

No discarded leaves exist for this brief movement; nor are there any deleted passages within the composition draft itself.

VI Libera me

An early draft of the opening of the movement (fol. 93^r) survives in which the choral entries do not follow the shape of the final version, although the percussion/string march is present virtually in its ultimate shape. In the published version of this passage the choral line (built around semitones) relates more clearly to earlier symmetries within the piece. Britten made several attempts at the soprano's 'Tremens' passage, the earliest having a waltz-like orchestral accompaniment (fol. 94^r–94^v). The reprise of the 'Dies irae, dies illa' was also subjected to some reconsideration, whereas the final, long Owen setting ('Strange Meeting') appears to have troubled Britten very little.

Full score

The full score of the *War Requiem* (*GB–Lbl* Add. MS No. 60610, on loan to the Britten–Pears Library) comprises 137 folios of 34-stave manuscript paper (Schirmer Imperial Brand No. 14), measuring 44.7 x 34 cm., bound in leather boards. Following the usual pattern for a Britten full score of this type, the manuscript is in more than one hand. The clefs, bar lines, instrument names and vocal lines appear in the hands of two copyists (Imogen Holst and Rosamund Strode, who was to succeed Miss Holst as Britten's music assistant in 1963) who worked from the composition draft and vocal score ahead of the composer, while the instrumentation is in Britten's hand throughout. As far as the 'Libera me' the copyists' work can be easily distinguished from the composer's, as they wrote in black ink while he retained his favoured pencil. In the final movement, however, pressures of looming deadlines may have forced the use of pencil by both copyists.[14]

The dedicatees

Apart from the title and list of movements, the prelims of the composition draft include the epigraph taken from Owen's preface to his poems ('My subject is War, and the pity of War./ The Poetry is in the pity... / All a poet can do today is warn') and on the title-page (fol. 2ʳ) a different, rather fuller, dedication to the one subsequently included in the published score: 'In Commemoration of all the Fellow-Sufferers of the Second World War, & in loving memory of Roger Burney..., Piers Dunkerley..., David Gill..., Michael Halliday...' In the published score Britten omits the reference to the 'Fellow-Sufferers', possibly fearing that his own acknowledged status during the war as a pacifist and conscientious objector might open the way for criticism of his identifying with 'genuine' sufferers. Instead, he chose to commemorate four young men, all friends, three of whom were killed in action during the 1939–45 conflict; the fourth, Piers Dunkerley, whom everyone assumes to have died in the war,[15] in fact committed suicide in 1959, while the *War Requiem* was being planned. Snapshots of each of the dedicatees were found together in an envelope in the Red House, Britten and Pears's Aldeburgh home, after Pears's death in 1986; the photographs had clearly belonged to the composer.

Roger Burney (1919–42) was more a friend of Pears's than of Britten's; rather like the eponymous character Owen Wingrave in Britten's pacifist opera, he was born into a military family and became a convinced pacifist; however, he changed his views after a palpable German atrocity. He enlisted in the Royal Naval Volunteer Reserve and while on active service in 1941 he visited New York,[16] where Britten and Pears were then living. As the British Navy Liaison Officer on the French submarine *Surcouf*, he died when the vessel was lost with all hands in February 1942.[17]

David Gill was a cousin of the Reeve family in Lowestoft (Basil Reeve was one of Britten's closest boyhood friends) who occasionally stayed with his relatives when on holiday from St Paul's Cathedral choir school. (In 1933 he had sung through part of *A Boy was Born* for the composer.) Gill had been killed in action in the Mediterranean. While working on the *War Requiem* in 1961, Britten wrote to Gill's mother:

Although he was a bit younger than I, I was very fond of him, and he helped a great deal by singing over music I had written. I am engaged on a big work now for the re-opening of Coventry Cathedral, a War Requiem, and I wish to inscribe it to several of my friends who were killed in this last terrible war. I was very shocked when I heard later that David had been one of these, and I wonder if you would allow me to write his name with the others, as a tribute, at the head of the Requiem.

Michael Halliday had been a schoolboy at Britten's old prep school, South Lodge (1923–7), who (according to John Pounder, another close boyhood

friend of Britten's) was 'rather an odd sort of character – lonely and sad ...
he always seemed rather an outsider until Ben took him in hand, and looked
after him'.[18] During the 1930s he was in the merchant navy and continued to
keep in touch with the composer. He went missing in 1944.[19]

The last of the dedicatees, Piers Dunkerley (1921–59), was, like Halliday,
a pupil at South Lodge (1930–4). During the 1930s Britten and Dunkerley
kept up a regular correspondence and it was to Britten that Dunkerley often
turned for advice. On leaving school he joined the Royal Marines, during the
war serving as captain; he was wounded and taken prisoner during the 1944
Normandy landings. After the war he continued his career as a professional
soldier and remained intermittently in touch with Britten. In the late 1950s
he returned to civilian life (he found employment with a firm of coal
merchants) and was engaged to be married. Dunkerley's marriage plans fell
through and it was this disappointment, perhaps, coupled with difficulties in
accommodating himself to civilian life after so many years in the armed
forces, that led to his tragic suicide in June 1959.[20]

3

The musical language: idiom and structure

By the nineteenth century, musical settings of the Latin Requiem Mass had developed out of all recognition from their modest polyphonic origins in the Renaissance. Requiem settings had first begun to flourish after the *Missa pro defunctis* became an established element of the Roman liturgy under Pius V in 1570, although during the seventeenth century they cultivated a musical idiom characterized by deliberate conservatism. With Mozart and the subsequent rise of romanticism this restraint yielded to a new desire for musical innovation and the communication of strong emotions, and the Requiem became a vehicle for subjectivity and musical dramatization just as much as any other genre in the nineteenth century. The 'Dies irae' (the text of the Requiem's Sequence, often omitted by earlier composers) now became the focal point of musical settings, its vivid imagery inspiring Berlioz and others to unprecedented heights of orchestrational virtuosity and ferocity. Verdi's famous and highly dramatic treatment of the 'Dies irae' in his Requiem of 1874 was part of a long tradition established by contributions to the genre from the pens of Mozart (1791), Cherubini (1816) and Berlioz (1837). Like these three forebears, Verdi drew on his experience as an opera composer in creating a response to the Requiem text noted for its musico-dramatic flair. Hans von Bülow famously described the work as 'Verdi's latest opera, in ecclesiastical dress';[1] significantly, many early performances of the Verdi Requiem took place in opera houses.

To a certain degree, von Bülow's remark may also be applied to Britten's *War Requiem*. By the time of its composition in 1961, Britten had completed no fewer than ten operas and there can be little doubt that his interest in the Requiem text sprang more from an awareness of its dramatic possibilities than from a keen interest in liturgical observance. As we shall see, his musical response to the Latin words bears all the hallmarks of the sophisticated musico-dramatic techniques he had evolved in the course of his development as a composer of stage works. More surprising, perhaps, is an explicit debt to Verdi's example, amply demonstrated by a number of musical parallels between the *War Requiem* and Verdi's Requiem first noted in an article by Malcolm Boyd published in 1968.[2]

In an interview conducted shortly after Boyd's article appeared, Donald Mitchell asked Britten if he had been conscious of historical precedents during work on the *War Requiem*. Britten's uncharacteristically 'roundabout' reply (to use the composer's own phrase) concluded:

I think that I would be a fool if I didn't take notice of how Mozart, Verdi, Dvořák – whoever you like to name – had written their Masses. I mean, many people have pointed out the similarities between the Verdi *Requiem* and bits of my own *War Requiem*, and they may be there. If I have not absorbed that, that's too bad. But that's because I'm not a good enough composer, it's not because I'm wrong.[3]

In being aware of earlier contributions to the genre with which he was preoccupied, Britten was doing no more than adopting an approach identical to that which had coloured the score of his ballet *The Prince of the Pagodas* (1956) with frequent and affectionate stylistic echoes of earlier Russian ballet masters such as Tchaikovsky, Stravinsky and Prokofiev. The allusions to Verdi in the *War Requiem* are, however, more specific and sufficiently widespread (one commentator has even found them 'disturbing': see p. 87) to warrant closer investigation.

Like Verdi's, Britten's text-setting is characterized by an awareness of the possibilities offered by the words themselves for the direct communication of emotion. Both composers set the opening choral repetitions of the words 'Requiem aeternam' to syllabic rhythmic patterns in a subdued atmosphere of expectancy. In setting the 'Dies irae' both composers show a fondness for the simple but effective dramatic impact achieved by inserting rests between individual words or even syllables, a technique which caused some consternation amongst critics attending an early performance of Verdi's Requiem at London's Royal Albert Hall; the reviewer for the *Morning Post* declared that 'the breaking of [the] words into short, sharp ejaculations, like a series of barks or yells, is certainly not indicative of reverence'.[4] Rhythmic similarities between the two works extend to the use of dotted rhythms for 'Rex tremendae majestatis' in the 'Dies irae', and the appearance of a rhythmic pattern identical to Verdi's for 'Tremens factus sum ego' in the 'Libera me' (Ex. 3.1). The echo of Verdi in Ex. 3.1b is strengthened by the appearance of a chromatic melodic line immediately after the rhythm in question. In both Verdi's and Britten's 'Agnus Dei', choir and orchestra combine in a low-tessitura pianissimo melody in unharmonized octaves. But by far the most overt correspondences between the two Requiems occur in

Ex. 3.1

(a) Verdi

[Moderato]

Soprano

Tre - mens   fa - ctus   sum   e - go   et   ti - - - - me - o,

(b) Britten

[Quicker]

Soprano

Tre - mens...   fac - tus...   sum   e - go...   e - go...   et   ti - - - - me - o. ___

the settings of the 'Dies irae'. Britten's choice of Verdi's key (G minor) for this movement must surely have been intentional, and the use of prominent off-beat bass-drum strokes (cf. three bars after Britten's Fig. 21) supports the parallel. As Boyd noted, both composers set the 'Liber scriptus' to melodies for soprano solo centred on a perfect fifth from A to E.[5] The most striking connection, however, is demonstrated by Britten's 'Lacrimosa': like Verdi's, his is set in B flat minor with prominent sharpened fourth (see Ex. 3.2), and both composers begin this section by allocating the melodic line to their soprano soloists.

Parallels between Britten and Verdi extend beyond these localized similarities to embrace longer-term structural procedures. Verdi makes three recapitulations of his G minor 'Dies irae' material, two at later points in the same movement (after the 'Liber scriptus' and before the 'Lacrimosa') and the third in the course of the 'Libera me' where the liturgical text itself recapitulates the phraseology of the 'Dies irae'. Britten twice recapitulates his G minor 'Dies irae' material: like Verdi, he returns to it immediately before the 'Lacrimosa' (and since this repetition of the text is non-liturgical, it must have been prompted by Verdi's innovation), and then follows his example in matching the 'Libera me' allusion to the 'Dies irae' text with an appropriate musical recapitulation.

In order to appreciate the most compelling explanation for the presence of these direct allusions to Verdi in the *War Requiem*, it is necessary to examine the complex musical context in which they are found. With the single and

Ex. 3.2

(a) **Verdi**

(b) **Britten**

important exception of the Verdi influence, the *War Requiem* is without doubt a highly original reworking of the genre, breaking new artistic ground in its daring juxtaposition of vernacular poems and Latin liturgical texts, and the bleak portrayal of man's inhumanity offered by the Owen poems seriously undermines the stylized religious phrases of condolence and consolation voiced by the words of the *Missa pro defunctis*. Britten allocates the latter almost exclusively to a soprano soloist, mixed chorus and full orchestra, while reserving some Latin passages for a distant chorus of boys' voices supported by chamber organ. Against this broad musical background are offset the Owen poems, brilliantly vital texts in English conveyed with considerable immediacy in virtuoso settings for tenor and baritone soloists (representing in the final song two soldiers from opposing armies)[6] and accompanied by a twelve-piece instrumental ensemble corresponding to that which Britten had exploited with such success in the chamber operas *The Rape of Lucretia* (1946), *Albert Herring* (1947) and *The Turn of the Screw* (1954). It has often been noted that Britten reserves his characteristic instrumental ingenuity for the intimacy of the Owen settings, cultivating a more conventional and grandiose approach to orchestration in the Latin passages where prolonged instrumental doublings untypical of the composer are the norm (e.g. the long melodic paragraphs of the 'Requiem aeternam' or the widespread doublings of the choral fugue in the 'Offertorium'). It is significant that Britten's allusions to Verdi are exclusively to be found in the Latin sections with full orchestra where, as Boyd comments, they 'serve as terms of reference for the listener, helping to form a familiar background against which certain disruptive elements in Owen's verses ... may stand out more forcefully'.[7]

In many respects the *War Requiem* marked the culmination of Britten's middle-period style, synthesizing many aspects of his earlier music and exploring them so exhaustively that a marked change of stylistic direction in the works which were to follow it was something of an inevitability. (With the exception of the modestly dimensioned *Cantata Misericordium*, which treated a further compassionate topic by way of postscript to the *War Requiem* in 1963, Britten's output in the 1960s cultivated a sparse and highly economical idiom hinted at in the Requiem only by elusive passages such as the closing bars of the 'Sanctus' and the celebrated restraint of 'Strange Meeting'.) Because of its 'encyclopaedic quality',[8] therefore, echoes of earlier Britten works not surprisingly abound in the pages of the Requiem. We saw earlier (p. 12) how the Spanish Civil War piece *Ballad of Heroes* (1939) utilized the spatial separation of instrumental groups to throw the distant, militaristic trumpet fanfares into relief, and this work had also mingled orchestral melody-based textures with solo vocal recitative. The savagely ironic 'dances of death' which Britten created for youthful politically orientated works such as *Our Hunting Fathers* (1936), the *Ballad of Heroes* and (in its 'Dies irae') the *Sinfonia da Requiem* (1940) are recalled by the grimly spirited setting of Owen's 'The Next War' in the 'Dies irae'. The *Sinfonia da Requiem*, itself conceived as a pacifist statement in the midst of the Second World War (see p. 14), suggests a number of parallels with Britten's later Requiem: the first movement ('Lacrymosa') is close to the 'Requiem aeternam' of the *War Requiem* in both tonality and melodic profiles, the central scherzo ('Dies irae') is centred on the interval of a tritone (see below) and incorporates vigorous brass fanfares in triplet rhythms which look directly ahead to those in the later 'Dies irae', while the third movement ('Requiem aeternam') commences with prominent bass clarinet and harp doubling – a sonority recalled at the words 'Let us sleep now...' in the *War Requiem* ('Libera me', Fig. 127).[9] Britten was experienced at handling the 14-line sonnet form preferred by Owen (see p. 101, note 12) well before embarking on the Requiem, having composed two song-cycles to texts exclusively in this form by Michelangelo and Donne in 1940 and 1945 respectively. His *Canticle II: Abraham and Isaac*, composed in 1952, had treated a subject of vital relevance to both the Latin and Owen texts used in the 'Offertorium', and for the latter Britten drew heavily and ironically on the canticle's musical material (see pp. 67–8 below). The 1959 *Missa Brevis* for boys' voices and organ (composed concurrently with work on the Requiem) provided a convenient study for the musical idiom of the remote boys' choir.

Certain passages of the score demonstrate Britten's artistically fruitful involvement with Asian cultures, most notably the gamelan music of Bali which he had recently appropriated to his own ends in *The Prince of the Pagodas* while still under the spell of a visit to Indonesia in 1956.[10] The ritualistic accelerating rhythms for tuned percussion at the beginning of the 'Sanctus' (examined on p. 70 below) provide the clearest example of oriental influence, being found both in gamelan music and in the Japanese court music (Gagaku) which Britten had also explored in 1956. Elsewhere, techniques redolent of the gamelan have become a natural extension of Britten's style. The sporadic gong punctuation throughout the 'Requiem aeternam' recalls the schemes of colotomic (i.e. 'dissecting') punctuation provided in gamelan music by the lowest gongs in the ensemble; hetero-phonic blurring between voices and brass is employed in the two 'Hosanna' sections of the 'Sanctus' to create the illusion of a highly resonant acoustic;[11] and the tranquillity of the closing 'Let us sleep now...' is largely created by a static pentatonicism. The most hauntingly memorable instrumental sonority in the work is that of tolling tubular bells, Britten's fondness for this instrument having surfaced in many earlier works as part of the fascination for tuned percussion instruments which undoubtedly intensified the allure held for him by the gamelan. Shortly before Britten began the *War Requiem* he had renewed his acquaintance with pseudo-gamelan sonorities in the opera *A Midsummer Night's Dream* (1960), where they had been used to promote the orchestrational contrasts characterizing the three distinct groups of characters participating in the drama; this recent experience must have proved beneficial in tackling a similar juggling of three contrasting idioms (now intensified by spatial separation) in the Requiem.

Most of the compositional techniques evolved by Britten to provide a subtle musical commentary on the stage action in his operatic works are encountered in the *War Requiem*, although the directness with which the work's didactic message is conveyed results in a generally simpler application of methods which in earlier operas had been utilized with notable complexity and sophistication. Thus, for instance, motivic manipulation in the Requiem is clear-cut, the principal thematic ideas tending to recur without any attempt to disguise them. In this respect the *War Requiem* is closer to the 1953 coronation opera *Gloriana* (which explores a comparable dichotomy between public responsibility and private anxieties, and is designedly direct in the simplicity of its thematic cross-references) than to works such as *Billy Budd* or *The Turn of the Screw*, both of which embody a complex network of subtle motivic allusions. The tonal structures on which the music of the Requiem is based are clearly defined and, for the most part, do not carry the weight of dramatic symbolism with which they are frequently entrusted in the operas. (A few important exceptions will be noted in the course of the commentary below.) As in earlier scores, most notably *A Midsummer Night's Dream*,[12] Britten explores the fruitful tension between fully chromatic writing and diatonic harmony throughout the work. Twelve-note collections are used to symbolize the universe of heaven and earth (see p. 70) and affirmative triadic progressions sometimes encompass all twelve roots (see p. 61). But highly chromatic passages such as the twelve-note dissolution of an already rarefied texture at the end of the 'Sanctus' remain isolated incidents, decorating rather than subverting an overall tonal framework solidly founded on clear tonal centres.

As already shown, Britten emphasizes the distinction between (and implied incompatibility of) his full-blown settings of the stereotyped religious sentiments of the Latin Mass and the chamber-orchestral treatment of the Owen texts partly by a contrast between a conventional Verdi-inspired idiom and a flexible, virtuoso approach to instrumentation and text-setting in the passages for tenor and baritone soloists. At a further remove from these two distinct musical planes lie the boys' voices, which intone 'the impassive calm of a liturgy that points beyond death'.[13] The boys are isolated from the other performers not only by virtue of physical separation, but also by Britten's cultivation of a pseudo-archaic idiom for them (redolent of certain passages in the contemporaneous *Missa Brevis*) which lends further remoteness and inaccessibility to the messages of prayer and salvation they attempt to convey. Allusions to the melodic style of mediaeval plainsong are ubiquitous in their thematic material, which tends to move by step within the restricted range of a third, fourth or fifth (see Ex. 3.3). This chant-like style also appears on occasion in the full chorus (cf. the soprano line in the 'Kyrie', quoted in Ex. 3.9). Successions of parallel fourths or fifths reminiscent of mediaeval *organum* invade the music for soprano, choir and full orchestra at those moments when Britten wishes to emphasize the remoteness and historical inappropriateness of the religious concepts expressed. They occur most obviously in the 'Benedictus' (Ex. 3.4), where the archaic flavour is reinforced by Britten's favourite Lydian sharpened fourth, but are also to be found in the 'Offertorium' (at Figs. 68 and 83) where they serve to punctuate the close of the two fugal sections. A tellingly ironic use of *organum* fourths occurs in the 'Agnus Dei' when the tenor sings of priests flawed by pride (nine bars after Fig. 97), alluding to the complacency of conventional religious attitudes implied elsewhere in the Requiem. The only other occurrence of deliberate archaism in the Owen settings is equally ironic: in 'The Parable of the Old Man and the Young' ('Offertorium', Fig. 74), the simultaneous recitation for the two male soloists on the perfect fourth A–D for the words of the angel who attempts to intercede on behalf of the doomed Isaac sounds as remote and unearthly as the exhortations of the distant boys' voices. The angel's injunction is ignored by Abraham, who proceeds to slay his son 'and half the seed of Europe, one by one'.

With such potentially rich and varied resources at his disposal, Britten clearly needed some means of creating internal musical cohesion which would allow him to interrelate the idioms of the three performing groups effectively. With an inspired simplicity entirely typical of his compositional genius, he chose a single interval for this task: the augmented fourth (tritone). Quite apart from its role as an abstract unifying device which permeates the music on a local level as well as governing long-term tonal planning, this instantly recognizable and invariably disquieting interval serves to symbolize the essentially ambiguous and unresolved nature of the *War Requiem*'s message, of which more will be said below. While agreeing with Peter Evans that 'the frequent appearance of so primary an element

Ex. 3.3

(a)

(b)

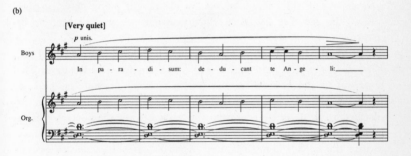

Ex. 3.4

Ex. 3.5

should discourage us from attaching too limitedly programmatic or "dramatic" a significance to it',[14] it is important to note that its frequent association with the concept of *requiem* ('rest', and presumably therefore 'peace') suggests that any peace which mankind may attain is likely to be uneasy and inconclusive.

The tritone is frequently heard in isolation (Ex. 3.5a; cf. also Exx. 3.7 and 3.20), as in the bells and choir at the very beginning of the Requiem. The choice of C and F sharp as the focal pitches throughout the piece is intriguing. Deryck Cooke astutely pointed out that many composers in the nineteenth and twentieth centuries who wished to use the interval with its original sinister connotation of *diabolus in musica* tended to alight on those pitches which had been introduced to correct the 'flaws' caused by the occurrence of this interval within the diatonic major scale. F sharp and B flat were first introduced in the Middle Ages to cancel out the augmented fourth F–B in the diatonic scale of C, and Cooke argued that composers instinctively revert either to the pitches of the 'flaw' itself (F–B) or to the two historical 'corrections' (C–F sharp and E–B flat) when singling out tritones for special treatment.[15]

As well as presenting it in simple isolation, Britten also uses the tritone in a number of different guises. It may be partitioned into two minor thirds to create diminished triads (Ex. 3.5b, which shows how two different diminished triads may be encompassed by the same two pitches), the harmonic device he was later to use as a symbol for war in the overtly pacifist opera *Owen Wingrave* (1970). A characteristic example of Britten's use of diminished triads is to be found at the start of the 'Dies irae' (Ex. 3.10) where they undermine the stability of the major triads of the militaristic fanfares. The tritone may also be partitioned into the three whole-tone steps from which it derives its name, and thus form half of a whole-tone scale (Ex. 3.5c). Patterns

Ex. 3.6

based on this whole-tone segment occur too frequently to list, but particularly clear examples occur in the boys' melody from the 'Requiem aeternam' (Ex. 3.6a) and in the descending trombone scales of the 'Dies irae' (Ex. 3.6b). Lastly, these three whole-tone steps also form the first four notes of the Lydian mode (Ex. 3.5d), which Britten habitually uses throughout his *œuvre* as a symbol for peace or innocence. Among the many textually appropriate applications of this mode in the *War Requiem* are the appearance of the angel in 'The Parable of the Old Man and the Young', where F sharp inflections colour the prevailing C major, and the closing 'Let us sleep now…', which progresses from its initial pentatonicism to the Lydian mode on D.

The *War Requiem* is subdivided into six movements[16] which strictly preserve the sequence of texts comprising the Proper and Ordinary of the Latin Requiem Mass. The opening movement ('Requiem aeternam') corresponds to the Introit and succeeding 'Kyrie', the second ('Dies irae') forms the Sequence, the third ('Offertorium') the Offertory, the fourth combines 'Sanctus' and 'Benedictus', while the fifth comprises the 'Agnus Dei'. The latter is here distinct from the standard Mass version of the text in its substitution of 'Dona eis requiem' for 'Miserere nobis', and 'Dona eis requiem sempiternam' for 'Dona nobis pacem': Britten's use of the latter for the final tenor solo phrase is therefore a deliberate and poignant departure from the liturgical Requiem text (see p. 36). The final movement ('Libera me') is the Responsory of Absolution drawn from the burial service. Nine poems by Wilfred Owen are strategically sited within this six-part scheme, one in each movement apart from the lengthy 'Dies irae' which contains no fewer than four. The ironies thrown up by Britten's carefully calculated

Ex. 3.7

juxtaposition of English and Latin texts are explored in the course of the following synoptic commentary.

I Requiem aeternam

To the accompaniment of tolling bells which punctuate statements of a 'slow and solemn' orchestral theme later to become significant, the choir tentatively intones its plea for eternal rest and perpetual light to be granted to the souls of the departed. Within the first twenty bars, Britten establishes a tonal scheme which will govern substantial parts of the remainder of the Requiem. The two pitches of the omnipresent tritone are first given out individually, F sharp by the sopranos and tenors followed by C from the altos and basses, each pitch reinforced by bell strokes. Then, at the first climax in dynamics, the two pitches are rapidly juxtaposed (Ex. 3.7) above the dominant pedal A which underpins this D minor section. Emphasis on the dominant note of prevailing keys is typical of Britten's tonal handling throughout the work, but here the triple conjunction of A, F sharp and C is especially significant: they not only comprise a diminished triad (cf. Ex. 3.5b) but, as part of a dominant-seventh chord in G minor, they pull towards the key of the subsequent 'Dies irae'. This function of the tritone C–F sharp as part of G minor is later made explicit towards the end of the work during the setting of Owen's 'Strange Meeting' (see Exx. 3.19 and 3.20). Throughout the choral passages of the 'Requiem aeternam' the choir is restricted to these two pitches, and their F sharps conflict in uneasy false relations with the F naturals of the D minor towards which the orchestral melody constantly pulls.

With a sudden shift to a sprightly tempo, the distant boys' voices enter for 'Te decet hymnus' with a highly chromatic melody (each phrase built from eleven different notes). The accompanying sequence of pure triads in the chamber organ contrasts with the elusive harmonic vocabulary of the preceding orchestral music, but the triads swiftly exhaust all twelve possible roots. Britten's use of simple twelve-note propositions such as this is generally reserved for portions of the Latin text referring to God's grandeur and omnipotence (cf. p. 70 below). Throughout this passage an audible link with the previous choral music is maintained by inverted pedal points in the orchestral violins which alternate between C and F sharp, each of the boys' vocal phrases beginning and ending on a triad containing one of these two pitches. As the boys' voices fade into the distance, their melodic shapes fill in the whole-tone steps between the same two notes (Ex. 3.6a) and come to rest on them in isolation, neatly dovetailing with the re-entry of the chorus and orchestra for a compressed and modified restatement of the opening section.

The enharmonic equivalence between F sharp and G flat allows Britten to sideslip into B flat minor[17] for the entry of the tenor solo and chamber orchestra in the first Owen setting, 'Anthem for Doomed Youth'. This celebrated poem, described by its author as one of his two best war poems (see p. 7), immediately undermines the hopes expressed by the chorus, bemoaning the futility of conventional religion in mourning the death of a soldier in battle. Owen catalogues a host of ecclesiastical details – passing-bells, orisons, prayers, choirs, candles, pall and flowers (the 'abominations of desolation' referred to by the poet in the letter to his mother quoted on pp. 2–3). Britten is quick to seize on the irony created by locating such a provocative text early in the Requiem and immediately transforms the luminous tritone of the orchestral bells into a nervously brittle and etiolated harp tremolo on the same pitches as the tenor bitterly declaims 'What passing-bells for these who die as cattle?' This is one of the most unsettling moments in the entire work (with an effect quite out of proportion to the

Ex. 3.8

[Very quick and agitated]

simplicity of the means employed), and it sets the tone for the disturbing ironies explored by Britten's later juxtaposition of English and Latin texts.

Much of the musical material in this setting of 'Anthem for Doomed Youth' will recur later in the Requiem. The tenor soloist prolongs the emphasis on the tritonal pitches C and G flat (especially prominent in his melisma on 'prayers'), while the strings develop an animated theme (Ex. 3.8, derived from the orchestral melody which began the movement) which will become significant in the 'Libera me'. Owen's 'shrill, demented choirs of wailing shells' are portrayed by flute and clarinet,[18] and the battlefield is further suggested by horn fanfares; both ideas will be reused in later movements as martial imagery. When the text avers that the 'holy glimmers of good-byes' will be seen in the eyes of boy acolytes rather than in the candles they hold, Britten brings back the melody of the boys' choir's 'Te decet hymnus' with its wide-ranging triadic accompaniment.

The brief, almost epigrammatic, setting of the 'Kyrie' for unaccompanied choir punctuated by bell strokes which concludes this movement offers little consolation after the disturbing implications of the Owen poem. Each of the three choral phrases commences with the bells' tritone C (= B sharp)–F sharp; the first two phrases return to these pitches but the third cadences chromatically onto a chord of F major (Ex. 3.9). F has been prepared in advance by its appearance during the 'Te decet hymnus' and as a pedal note at the end of the Owen setting (Fig. 15), making the resolution appear logical enough. But when this 'Kyrie' returns in modified forms twice more, at the end of the 'Dies irae' and again at the end of the work as a whole, its final bar seems curiously inconclusive.

II Dies irae

The vivid liturgical picture of the Day of Judgement begins with a flurry of subdued triadic fanfares in the brass (Ex. 3.10), representing the calls of the battlefield as much as the Last Trump. They are soon to be transformed into a powerful climax of terror after the choir has hesitantly entered with scale

Ex. 3.9

figures in a limping septuple metre above a dominant pedal in the Verdian G minor (see p. 51 above); the choral sections are interspersed with overlapping developments of two fanfare figures ('x' and 'y' in Ex. 3.10), concluding with versions of the brass scale in Ex. 3.6b. At Fig. 21 both choir and fanfares combine in a moment of climax before the texture dissipates in preparation for the next Owen poem.

The baritone soloist sings six lines from Owen's incomplete fragment 'Bugles sang' to a delicate accompaniment in the chamber orchestra derived from the fanfare motifs 'x' and 'y', beginning with a piquant superimposition of the two triads with which the 'Dies irae' commenced (G major and B flat major; cf. Ex. 3.10). Again Britten's motivic references are ironic, the bugles which are now 'saddening the evening air' and 'sorrowful to hear' being represented by subdued and etiolated versions of the material to which the blazing trumpets of the Apocalypse have just thrilled us. When the soloist sings of the 'shadow of the morrow weighed on men', a ponderous version of Ex. 3.6b is heard in the horn: this is immediately

Ex. 3.10

inverted to create a climactic ascent for the 'Voices of old despondency resigned'. The skilfully understated manipulation of the 'Dies irae' themes throughout this section provides an appropriate and economical portrait of a 'shadow of the morrow' which here implies a premonition of the Day of Judgement itself.

The baritone solo ends with the word 'slept', supported by an A major triad which affords a fleeting glimpse ahead to the A major/D Lydian tonality of the 'Let us sleep now...' with which the Requiem will ultimately conclude. The soprano soloist now makes her first entrance to music also based on A (for the echo of Verdi here, see p. 51 above), resuming the liturgical text in a fanfare-like declamation of 'Liber scriptus' accompanied by the woodwind and horns of the full orchestra. Above another dominant pedal (ominously repeated Es in the timpani) a semichorus answers with involuted chromaticism for the words 'Quid sum miser tunc dicturus?' – the first association of chromaticism with human wretchedness, an idea which will resurface with force in the final 'Libera me'. The soprano restates her fanfare in inversion (Fig. 31) and continues to sing the 'Rex tremendae majestatis' simultaneously with a reworking of the choir's chromaticism, now above a tonic pedal A in the timpani and concluding in an uneasy ambiguity between major and minor.

Immediately the mood changes to 'fast and gay' as the two male soloists combine for their spirited rendering of Owen's sonnet 'The Next War', the other of the two war lyrics singled out by the poet as his best. Owen originally headed his poem with the following epigram by Sassoon:

> War's a joke for me and you,
> While we know such dreams are true.

Here the irony resides in the image of two jaunty soldiers walking 'quite friendly up to Death', whom they treat as their 'old chum', openly laughing in the face of the awe-inspiring image of the powerful and remote arbiter of human mortality portrayed in the preceding liturgical passage by the soprano and semichorus. The setting is a concise ternary structure, still with A as its tonic but migrating to C in the central section for a splendidly blasé melody sung by the two voices in unison at

> We chorussed when he sang aloft;
> We whistled while he shaved us with his scythe.

In the bustling accompaniment to these words, the horn's bugle call from 'Anthem for Doomed Youth' (Fig. 12) is recapitulated in combination with shrieking chromatics on high wind and violins representing the soldiers' manic whistling and subtly alluding to the choral setting of 'Quid sum miser'.

For the next portion of liturgical text, Britten divides his chorus into separate groups of female and male voices which remain distinct. The sopranos and altos sing the 'Recordare' in four-part imitation, built up over lilting ostinato patterns in the lower strings anchored on a pedal C: before each successive vocal part enters, the previous phrase culminates in a prominent descent through the three whole-tone steps of the scale segments in Ex. 3.5c. The final and highest entry, at the words 'Qui Mariam absolvisti', is in the Lydian mode used elsewhere to symbolize innocence or purity. From Fig. 45 until the next Owen setting the voices heard are exclusively male, a restriction helping to promote a martial atmosphere which will soon explode into the movement's grandest climax. Tenors and basses, at first heard independently but then with their melodies superimposed (a favourite Britten scheme), contrast the images of the damned consigned to the flames of Hell and the weeping suppliants remaining on earth.

In a thrilling surge, the music spills directly into the baritone's chillingly stark delivery of Owen's 'Sonnet: On Seeing a Piece of Our Artillery Brought into Action'. Once more, bitter irony is created by Owen's religious imagery which sees the gun as 'towering toward Heaven, about to curse' (not pray). Britten reduces Owen's original text to just six of its most striking lines, and ensures that the baritone ends no fewer than four of them with emphatic tritones mocking the earlier association of this interval with the pleading for 'requiem aeternam'. The suitably blunt accompaniment is a combination of hammered-out timpani broken chords and simple sustained triads rising by step (inevitably recalling the boys' 'Te decet hymnus' from the first movement). Britten derives the pounding timpani figures from the basses' 'Confutatis maledictis' in the preceding section: Owen's image of the great gun's shells beating down 'that arrogance which needs thy harm ... before its sins grow worse' is thereby explicitly linked with the earlier liturgical description of sinners roasting in the underworld. The six lines are

Ex. 3.11

(a)

The kind old sun __ will know.

(b)

Was it __ for this __ the clay grew tall? __

punctuated by interjections from the orchestral trumpets based on the fanfares of Ex. 3.10 and invariably conflicting sharply with the prevailing harmonies. This is the first time the main orchestral forces have invaded the music for chamber orchestra, and on their final entry the trumpets rapidly usher in a fortissimo recapitulation of the choral 'Dies irae' – a fittingly violent response to the baritone's concluding wish 'May God curse thee, and cut thee from our soul!'

In this restatement of the 'Dies irae', the music moves from its original G minor to a new key-area in preparation for the soprano solo's imploring 'Lacrimosa' (Ex. 3.2b) with its discreet choral accompaniment built from the same disjointed rhythms in septuple metre used earlier to characterize the more barbaric portions of the Latin text. The line 'Qua resurget ex favilla' ('when [mankind] will rise up again from the ashes')[19] is the cue for the next Owen setting, the bleak poem 'Futility' (Owen's draft title had been 'Frustration'). This text describes how a dead soldier is no longer revived by the 'kind old sun' which always used to wake him while he was still alive. Owen's despairing image is so closely linked to the liturgical text at this point that Britten punctuates the three sections of tenor recitative with continuing developments of Ex. 3.2b and ends two of the tenor's phrases with direct allusions to the soprano's melody (Ex. 3.11a recalls the 'Lacrimosa' and Ex. 3.11b the 'Qua resurget'). The chillingly negative conclusion

> – O what made fatuous sunbeams toil
> To break earth's sleep at all?

fizzles out on the tritone C–F sharp, heralding the return of the tolling bells from the 'Requiem aeternam' and the concluding choral setting of 'Pie Jesu'.

The latter reworks Ex. 3.9 and cadences once more onto an F major chord which here seems even remoter than on its first appearance.

III Offertorium

Although brief, the 'Offertorium' is the section of the *War Requiem* richest in irony. The centrepiece is Owen's 'Parable of the Old Man and the Young', which symbolically retells the story of Abraham and Isaac from Genesis 22. In Owen's version, Abraham binds his son 'with belts and straps' in the trenches of the First World War; when an angel calls him from heaven and enjoins him to sacrifice 'the Ram of Pride' in Isaac's stead, Abraham ignores him and proceeds to slay his son and 'half the seed of Europe, one by one'. By juxtaposing this text with the liturgical Offertory, which includes an invocation of God's promise to lead Abraham and his seed into holy light, Britten highlights one important level of irony. But a subtler and pervasive musical irony is created by the composer's substantial reworking of material borrowed from his own *Canticle II: Abraham and Isaac* (1952), a setting for alto, tenor and piano of the late fourteenth-century Chester Miracle Play based on the biblical tale.[20] The story must have appealed to the composer largely on account of its theme of the threatening of innocence (a recurrent preoccupation in his operatic output), and it carries a clear parallel with the Crucifixion: Abraham (whose name literally means 'father of the multitude') represents God the Father, while his innocent son Isaac is a willing sacrificial victim who even carries wood to the site of his impending death – just as Christ bore his own cross to Calvary. In the biblical story, the lamb which Isaac had assumed would become the burnt offering may itself be interpreted as a symbol for the Agnus Dei and associated with Christ crucified.[21]

The movement begins with the impassive chanting of the boys' choir quoted in Ex. 3.3a, and the sudden shift from a tonal centre of C sharp to an unequivocal G major for the choral fugue which follows is a good illustration of Britten's use of his seminal tritone to govern longer-term structural units. The fugue subject (Ex. 3.12a) is directly derived from Isaac's theme of sacrificial preparation in *Canticle II* (Ex. 3.12b), and is subjected to traditional contrapuntal techniques of inversion, stretto (including double stretto on simultaneous inversion and *recte* forms) and episodic fragmentation. Here Britten employs, for the only time in the Requiem, compositional techniques associated with this text in traditional Masses and oratorios. The chamber orchestra enters with a continuation of Ex. 3.12b above the

Ex. 3.12

(a)

[Lively]

Choir {T. / B.

Quam o - lim A - bra - hae pro - mi - si - sti, ___ et se - mi - ni e - - jus.

(b)

[Gently moving]

HERE ISAAC SPEAKETH TO HIS FATHER, AND TAKETH A BUNDLE OF STICKS AND BEARETH AFTER HIS FATHER.

Alto

Fa - ther, I am all rea - - - - - dy.

conflicting duplet rhythm with which it had been combined in the canticle, the theme adopting the whole-tone patterns of Ex. 3.5c and Ex. 3.6 as Owen's Isaac first addresses his father. The lush, almost romantic, tremolo accompaniment to his question about the identity of the sacrificial victim is borrowed from the canticle, as is the angular bassoon theme accompanying Abraham's preparations for the slaughter (Fig. 72). The latter had been used in the earlier work to signify Abraham's 'intent ever to be obedient' to God's commands. Fragments from the 'Dies irae' fanfares and the wailing shells of 'Anthem for Doomed Youth' recur as Abraham builds his trenches and parapets, and he stretches forth the knife to slay his son to a free inversion of Ex. 3.6b.

As the angel appears (Fig. 74), tenor and baritone soloists unite in a remarkable C major recitative borrowed from *Canticle II*, where a vocal duet had portrayed the words of God. In the canticle the duet had been in E flat major; Britten here transposes it not only to suit the lower registers of the different soloists, but also to correspond to other passages where this tonal centre is used to signify divine purity (cf. 'Qui Mariam absolvisti', Fig. 43). The serene C major chords outlined by strings and harp are made curiously luminous by their Stravinskian omission of the fifth, and the vocal recitation is deliberately archaic (see p. 56 above). As the angel indicates the Ram of Pride, Britten borrows a further melody from the canticle (Ex. 3.13) and achieves tonal symbolism of extraordinary subtlety. Within the Lydian-inflected C major at this point (which we have seen to symbolize purity) are contained the tritonal pitches C and F sharp (cf. Ex. 3.5d), a *diabolus in musica* corresponding to the sin of pride embodied in the Ram.

Ex. 3.13

After a flurry of semiquavers (Fig. 75, again borrowed from the canticle and outlining the harmonic contours of the angel's duet-recitative), the jaunty fugal theme (Ex. 3.12a) returns in E major as Abraham slays his son, pointedly adopting the angel's C major triad – alien to the new tonal context – as if in open defiance of his divine instructions. During sporadic repetitions of the final line ('half the seed of Europe, one by one'), implying that the destruction of Abraham's seed will continue for eternity, the distant boys' choir eerily intones 'Hostias et preces' in their customary archaic idiom, but now with harmonically disruptive accompaniment from the chamber organ. The gradual disintegration of the Owen setting and the boys' incantations continue to be superimposed in metrical non-alignment (a foretaste of the asynchrous procedures Britten was to cultivate in the church parables during the 1960s) until the choir and full orchestra re-enter to work their way mechanically through an oppressively muted and compressed recapitulation of the 'Quam olim Abrahae' fugue. Both texture and thematic shapes are strictly inverted from their first appearance and the music now polarizes around E minor rather than the original G major, thus completing the movement's coherent tonal scheme in which the tritonal opposition C sharp–G at the outset has been rationalized by the use of their closely linked relative keys: E major at the close of the Owen setting and E minor at the end of the movement.

IV Sanctus

The glittering accelerating tremolos scored for vibraphone, glockenspiel, antique cymbals, bells and piano which usher in the soprano soloist's 'Sanctus' (and for which Britten invented the notation ⅈⅉ) were clearly influenced by Indonesian gamelan music, as discussed on p. 54. Their prominent appearance at this point in the *War Requiem* may be explained in two different ways. First, they underline the sense of the enactment of a religious ritual and impart the hypnotic quality of an Eastern temple ceremony to the Western liturgy. Second, and more significantly, they echo the constant association in Britten's output between gamelan sonorities and unattainable goals. In later works, this connection was to be made still more explicit, with the gamelan sonorities in *Owen Wingrave* suggesting both the allure and essential remoteness of the peace towards which the eponymous hero strives, while in *Death in Venice* they represent the attractiveness of the Polish boy Tadzio and imply his fundamental incompatibility with Aschenbach. The *Wingrave* usage is directly prophesied in the present context, the percussion tremolos being pointedly restricted to the two tritonal pitches C and F sharp which have already been linked to the seemingly unattainable 'requiem aeternam'.

The full chorus, divided into eight parts, gradually enters in an extra-ordinary passage of unsynchronized chanting interpreted by Christopher Palmer as a borrowing from Holst's *Hymn of Jesus*.[22] In the space of fourteen bars all twelve pitches have been sounded in a chromatic totality graphically representing the text 'Pleni sunt coeli et terra gloria tua'.[23] The 'Hosanna' is then exultantly proclaimed to the accompaniment of blazing trumpets, firmly rooted in the traditional baroque ceremonial key of D major, before the music dies away and the soprano soloist re-enters with her restrained 'Benedictus' echoed by the chorus (Ex. 3.4).

A concise restatement of the triumphant 'Hosanna' yields immediately to a setting for baritone and chamber orchestra of Owen's 'The End'. (The first line of the poem, 'After the blast of lightning *from the East*' (my italics), may have originally suggested to Britten the idea of opening his 'Sanctus' with music of a distinctly oriental flavour.)[24] Familiar elements which reappear in the course of this setting include diminished triads (cf. Ex. 3.5b) and a tritone filled out with whole-tone steps (at 'all tears assuage'; cf. Ex. 3.5c). Tritonal relationships are emphasized at the climax, tonal centres of D and A flat being bitonally superimposed as the soloist questions 'white Age' about the likelihood of the dead being restored to life. The highly enigmatic replies are set in a disturbingly thin texture recalling Webern in its lucid pointillism and intervallic construction. The last five bars pass quickly through all twelve tones (the final three outlining a diminished triad) and the movement comes to rest on a low F sharp which serves as a dominant preparation for the B minor of the ensuing 'Agnus Dei'.

The sparseness of this ending to the 'Sanctus' (all the more effective in coming after the lush brilliance of the choral 'Hosanna') and the dispiriting message of the Owen poem makes this the bleakest moment in the *War Requiem*.[25] Significantly, it is tonally the most elusive part of the work.

V Agnus Dei

This minuscule but hauntingly beautiful movement marks a brief moment of repose and reflection before the traumatic onslaught of the ensuing 'Libera me'. It is the only section of the Requiem in which the Owen poetry and liturgical texts are in complete accord and, as if to emphasize their common ground, both chamber orchestra/tenor solo and full orchestra/choir are seamlessly alternated above a common ground-bass pattern. Owen's poem 'At a Calvary near the Ancre' develops an image explored by many First World War poets and painters: the presence of Christ on the modern battlefield, sustaining bodily wounds to atone for the sins of mankind. The liturgical plea to the Lamb of God to grant eternal rest to the departed constitutes an appropriate background to Owen's text.

The simplicity of the musical means which bind the Owen setting and choral 'Agnus Dei' together is entirely typical of Britten at his most powerful. The movement is based on falling and rising scale segments which revolve

Ex. 3.14

around the familiar tritonal poles of F sharp and C, now set in the context of a B minor with prominent Neapolitan or Phrygian inflections (Ex. 3.14). The tenor's melody begins by spanning the same tritone in falling whole-tone steps (cf. Ex. 3.5c and Ex. 3.6a), with the most expressive words of Owen's poem set as suspensions above the C major harmonies which occur in alternate bars. Thus 'hangs', 'disciples' and 'love' all appear on F sharp suspensions onto C major chords, a feature which not only emphasizes the focal tritone but constantly hints at the Lydian C modality used elsewhere to signify flawed purity; the word 'gentle' also occurs in a C major harmonization. Each orchestral paragraph ends with an extension of the rising C major scale followed by a whole-tone descent from C to F sharp before the ground-bass pattern of Ex. 3.14 returns. This expanded cadential figuration is adopted by the chorus (Ex. 3.15), and poignantly modified by the tenor solo in the final bars by reversing the order of F sharp and C with an unexpected inflection of C *minor* (Ex. 3.16). This non-liturgical textual addition on

Ex. 3.15

Choir (unison): do - na e - is re - qui - em.

Ex. 3.16

Tenor: Do - na no - bis pa - - - cem.

Britten's part (see p. 36) makes the plea for peace more explicit than at any other point in the Requiem.

VI Libera me

The funereal march which gradually evolves out of the murky opening of the Requiem's final and climactic movement bears something of a generic similarity to the mustering of the ship's complement to witness the execution in the final scene of *Billy Budd*, and is based on the string theme from 'Anthem for Doomed Youth' (Ex. 3.8). The theme is presented at first in a slow tempo as a mere rhythmic skeleton by the percussion, but it soon acquires pitches and rises inexorably up through the orchestral texture. The claustrophobic atmosphere of doom and destruction is here intensified by a return to the G minor of the 'Dies irae', and the march develops in a long-term accelerando towards the recapitulation of easily recognizable material from that movement between Figs. 110 and 116.

Britten masterfully builds up the tension towards this apocalyptic recapitulation, increasing the density of the choral counterpoint based on a sinuous chromatic motif (related to the 'Quid sum miser' of the 'Dies irae') which gradually unfolds above the orchestral march. As the tempo quickens by degrees, so the origins of Ex. 3.8 become more obvious: by Fig. 105 it has reached the same urgent tempo in which it was first presented in 'Anthem for Doomed Youth'. At this point, Britten alludes once more to the Verdi Requiem in a thematic parallel which also emphasizes the two diminished

Ex. 3.17

(a) **Britten**

(b) **Verdi**

triads based on C and F sharp (Ex. 3.17; cf. Ex. 3.5b). Beneath a further
reference to Verdi (Ex. 3.1) the 'Doomed Youth' theme moves into a rapid
triple metre, increasing the movement's heady momentum. The brass
fanfares from the 'Dies irae' are gradually reintroduced, surging in contrary
motion to create the most powerful dominant preparation encountered
anywhere in Britten's music (Ex. 3.18; note that the dominant eleventh here
includes the diminished triads of Ex. 3.17a). The recapitulation of the choral
'Dies irae' follows immediately and builds quickly to a shattering climax at
Fig. 116, the massive orchestral chord stiffened by the unexpected entry of
full organ. The G minor tonic triad is sustained in a long diminuendo as the
final statements of the 'Doomed Youth' and 'Libera me' themes die slowly
away to nothing.

The final Owen setting – 'Strange Meeting' – is both the longest and the
most economical in its restrained musical idiom. Its message of reconciliation
between friend and foe, in the eerie atmosphere of a subterranean cavern
after one has been killed by the other, transcends its ostensible surrealism to
create the simple statement of peace between all mankind to which every
musical event up to this point has tended. Significantly, Britten cut four lines
from Owen's poem (see p. 29), evidently uncomfortable with the realization
that this ultimate reconciliation was pictured by Owen as taking place in

Ex. 3.18

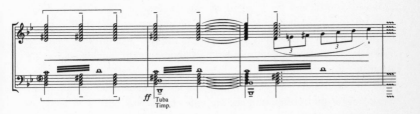

Hell; the composer fought shy of retaining these lines as a final bitter irony in the context of the impending 'In paradisum' with which the liturgy will conclude.

Throughout the tenor's opening recitative ('It seemed that out of battle I escaped'), a first-inversion G minor triad is almost inaudibly sustained by the chamber orchestra as a distant reminder of the battlefield which the climax of the 'Libera me' had portrayed. The vocal line alights on various tritonal patterns, and when the protagonist probes one of the lifeless corpses it springs up and stares at him to a surge from the strings on an incomplete dominant-seventh chord containing the tritone C–F sharp (Ex. 3.19). As the tenor addresses the enemy he has killed, the Requiem's principal tonal elements are encapsulated in a single bar (Ex. 3.20), the words 'Strange friend' set to the same tritone which here suggests the paradox of companionship between hunter and hunted. The baritone-enemy replies, lamenting the waste of life, hope and opportunity represented by his death, the

75

Ex. 3.19

preponderance of *perfect* fourths which shape his melodic lines signifying his resignation to his fate. (Britten has up to this point only stressed perfect – rather than augmented – fourths at dramatically corresponding moments, including the 'sad shires' and 'drawing-down of blinds' in 'Anthem for Doomed Youth', and the breaking of 'earth's sleep' at the end of the 'Dies irae'.) An eruption of fragmented fanfare reminiscences from the 'Dies irae' accompanies his passionate outcry against 'the pity war distilled', and the musical recapitulations continue with references to the rhythm of Ex. 3.8 (timpani) and the 'blasé' theme from 'The Next War' (see p. 65). The harmony wends its way back to the simple G minor triad heard at the beginning of the setting, and the baritone reveals his identity to his killer with understated directness.

By way of coda, the two soloists join forces to sing of their reconciliation and eternal rest ('Let us sleep now...') in a serene pentatonicism which is soon extended to embrace the Lydian mode on D. In the same tonality, although metrically unsynchronized, the boys' choir chants the 'In paradisum' (Ex. 3.3b), and their material is gradually taken over by the full chorus and orchestra. This unique conjoining of all the performing groups (spanning some forty-seven staves of full score, mostly subdued in dynamics), sharing the same music, serves as a fitting representation of the reconciliation with which the Owen setting ends.

It would have been tempting, and not uncathartic in effect, for Britten to have prolonged this serene *envoi* until the very closing bars of the *War Requiem*. But to do so would leave the listener far too comfortable, perhaps even complacent, about the fundamental issues, paradoxes and contradictions which this great work has addressed in the course of its eighty-five minutes. There are no clear-cut answers to the eternal problems of war and peace, and

Ex. 3.20

– as if to remind us of that disturbing fact – the final diatonic tutti is suddenly halted by the abrupt return of the tritone C–F sharp on tubular bells and a distant, passionless prayer for 'requiem aeternam' chanted by the distant boys to the same interval. The remaining forces twice attempt to restart their combined 'Let us sleep now...'/'In paradisum' but are twice more checked by the tonally disruptive bells. Defeated, almost dejected, the chorus adopts the familiar tritone and reverts to its elusively epigrammatic 'Kyrie' (Ex. 3.9) for the final 'Requiescant in pace', now shortened to two brief phrases and resolving the all-pervasive interval into that alien F major chord which seems to make the ending of the *War Requiem* so profoundly unsettling.

4

Critical reception

Any new *Requiem* setting has to compete with Verdi's and Fauré's and Mozart's treatment of the same words. Britten has approached the task in his own fresh and deeply felt way. It is not a *Requiem* to console the living; sometimes it does not even help the dead to sleep soundly. It can only disturb every living soul, for it denounces the barbarism more or less awake in mankind with all the authority that a great composer can muster. There is no doubt at all, even before next Wednesday's performance, that it is Britten's masterpiece.

This striking notice, appearing under the uncompromising headline 'Britten's masterpiece denounces war', was published in *The Times* on 25 May 1962 – five days before the first performance of the *War Requiem* in Coventry Cathedral. Although printed anonymously, the preview had been written by William Mann. Here was a leading critic of the day not only prepared to label the score as a 'masterpiece', but willing to do so even before a note of the music had been heard in public. His support for the *War Requiem* was still further intensified after the first performance. On 31 May he described it as 'the most masterly and nobly imagined work Britten has ever given us' and declared it to be 'so superbly proportioned and calculated, so humiliating and disturbing in effect, in fact so tremendous, that every performance it is given ought to be a momentous occasion'.

The warmly appreciative tone of Mann's articles was to be echoed in the vast majority of critical assessments attendant upon the première of the *War Requiem*. Indeed, it is difficult to call to mind any other major twentieth-century work which met with such instantaneous and unanimously high praise from almost all sectors of the media; praise which, one or two dissenting voices apart, has endured to the present day. Mann was by no means alone in his choice of 'masterpiece' as the most appropriate label, and Peter Evans sympathized with the composer for having been plunged into a predicament at once unfamiliar and daunting:

The knowledge that he has created an unrecognized masterpiece has been the perennial solace of the artistic nonentity. Yet we have now developed to so fine an art the faint praise reserved for the musical works of our contemporaries that the 'masterpiece' seems a concept of little meaning outside a hallowed but restricted area of music's past. So a work which is immediately accorded this title by both critical and popular acclaim ushers its composer into a niche that, however gratifying, cannot be comfortably familiar.

Benjamin Britten's *War Requiem* has stirred musical sensibilities in this country more powerfully than has any new work within recent memory...[1]

Entirely typical of the critical acclaim to which Evans refers were Peter Shaffer's remarks in his review for *Time & Tide* on 7 June 1962: 'I believe it to be the most impressive and moving piece of sacred music ever to be composed in this country, and one of the greatest musical compositions of the 20th century... I am at a loss to know how to praise the greatness of this piece of music.' He continued: 'the climax of this *War Requiem* is the most profound and moving thing which this most committed of geniuses has so far achieved. It makes criticism impertinent... Here the glorifying in technical skill is a sign of spiritual fulfilment in a brilliant artist.'

The work was first heard in London on 6 December 1962 at Westminster Abbey, at one of two highly successful performances in the capital during the winter of 1962–3. The immediate popularity enjoyed by the *War Requiem* with the listening public prompted Mann to resume his earlier theme in more detail:

The extraordinary popular success of Britten's *War Requiem* is something that has hardly happened to a new British composition since Elgar's first symphony broke on an astonished and delighted Edwardian London. There have been new works, Holst's *The Planets*, Ireland's piano concerto [!], several pieces of Vaughan Williams and Walton and Britten himself, that made a deep impression on devotees of contemporary English music and prompted several performances after the respectful première; but nothing to equal the flood of tickets to the two London performances of the *War Requiem* last month [December 1962] and this week.

There was never any doubt that the work deserved such a welcome, deserved to be heard and absorbed and pondered by everyone with a stake in the future, not to mention the immediate past history, of the world. It speaks directly and without compromise, in Britten's characteristic tone of voice and with a fierce originality and intensity that he has never before achieved; it speaks to us all and for us all...

The immediate impact of Britten's *War Requiem* is emotional, and herein lies a part of its immediate attraction for people who dismiss most modern music as an 'intellectual exercise' ... the art and craft by which we identify the mastery are only symptoms of the condition that our senses recognize on hearing this music – it is genuine, potent poetry...

We are confident of its abiding power because, below the surface of emotional intensity, there can be discerned a firm and coherent consistency of real musical invention that enwraps and supports the burden of the conception with pertinent points of reference at every level.[2]

That the 'immediate impact' of the work was one of emotional power had been eloquently demonstrated during rehearsals for the Coventry première when Dietrich Fischer-Dieskau, the baritone soloist, was moved to tears. In his autobiography, he recalled 'the first performance created an atmosphere of such intensity that by the end I was completely undone; I did not know where to hide my face. Dead friends and past suffering arose in my mind.'[3] (Fischer-Dieskau had been conscripted into the Wehrmacht in the closing stages of the Second World War while still a teenager.) Britten wrote to his librettist, William Plomer, on 5 June 1962: 'Poor F-Dieskau was so upset at the end that Peter couldn't get him out of the choir-stalls!'

The phenomenal success of the *War Requiem* continued apace. In January 1963 at Kingsway Hall, London, Britten conducted a recording of the work with the London Symphony Orchestra and Chorus which featured his original choice of vocal soloists: Pears, Fischer-Dieskau and Galina Vishnevskaya (the latter's part having been taken by Heather Harper in the early live performances) – each of the three representing a different combatant nation from the two world wars.[4] Not all went smoothly during the sessions. Vishnevskaya misinterpreted her physical separation from the two male soloists as discrimination and lay screaming on the floor in protest, unable to express herself in English; Britten was on the verge of being forced to record the work out of sequence when she suddenly and charmingly acquiesced without a word further being spoken on the matter.[5] Issued by Decca four months later, the recording (re-released on CD in 1985) sold nearly a quarter of a million copies in just five months. Sales were doubtless stimulated by the strikingly simple design of the boxed set, which printed the composer's name and the work's title in stark white capitals set against a jet-black background (a scheme conceived by Boosey & Hawkes for the covers of the published vocal and orchestral scores). The *Daily Mail* later noted that the double album headed the classical charts in a dozen countries; quick to seize on the commercial implications, it took evident glee in reporting the extent of the composer's growing financial gain from the work ('the *Requiem* is the highest point of a career that has made Britten one of the world's richest composers').[6] The recording was especially well received in Holland, where the work was first heard live in May 1963. An undated compilation of Dutch press cuttings at the Britten–Pears Library notes that two-thirds of the population of Holland had been exposed to publicity surrounding the *War Requiem* in national newspapers and periodicals, and makes quotation from twenty-five different reviews of the recording, unanimous in their praise. The phraseology recalls the powerful impact the work had already achieved in the United Kingdom, various critics hailing the score as 'one of the most superb anti-war monuments of our century', 'a masterpiece of strong dramatic allure' and 'an extraordinarily penetrating experience for everyone who has ears to hear' which had now been 'so perfectly immortalized on records by Decca's technicians, a miracle of beauty set in music'.

John Culshaw, who produced the Decca recording of the *War Requiem*, presented the composer with a unique fiftieth-birthday gift: an LP (of which, allegedly, only one copy was pressed) comprising highlights edited from Britten's sixteen hours of recording sessions, complete with the composer's comments from the rostrum recorded by a hidden microphone.[7] The disc was furnished with an authentic Decca label bearing the appropriate (if spurious) catalogue number 'BB50' and presented to the composer by Decca's managing director, Sir Edward Lewis, in an embossed leather sleeve. This imaginative gesture backfired somewhat when Britten took exception to what he felt had been an unwarranted invasion of privacy. The disc has survived, however, as an invaluable and fascinating testament to Britten's consummate abilities as a conductor.

With the *War Requiem* recording selling well, live performances attracted still more intense public interest. A performance at the 1964 Promenade Concerts, scheduled for 8 p.m. on 4 August to mark the exact fiftieth anniversary of Britain's declaration of war on Germany in 1914, was the first concert to sell out in that year's season. The Royal Albert Hall had proved itself to be better suited to the work's spatial design than Coventry Cathedral, the acoustics of the latter having caused some discomfort amongst listeners attending the première. Britten commented that he had designed the work 'for a big reverberant acoustic, and that is where it sounds best',[8] but several reviewers complained that much of the work's intricate detail was lost as a result. When given at the Royal Festival Hall on 12 December 1963 by the original interpreters (the only occasion on which the composer directed a live performance without an assistant conductor), the work not surprisingly suffered from the opposite problem: the Festival Hall's 'inappropriately clinical acoustic'[9] allowed unparalleled projection of detail but no sense of reverberation or of the spatial drama underlying the novel conception of the score. The Albert Hall had proved to be the best possible compromise when it hosted a performance on 9 January 1963 (the first occasion on which Vishnevskaya appeared as soprano soloist), and this venue has seen several of the work's most memorable interpretations in more recent years.

The universal relevance of the *War Requiem*'s pacifist message ensured the score an equally rapid acceptance outside the United Kingdom, especially in countries for which the two world wars had proved catastrophic. The first German performance took place in Berlin on 18 November 1962 (Armistice Day), Colin Davis standing in for an indisposed Britten to direct the Berlin Philharmonic Orchestra; Pears was joined by soloists Ella Lee and Walter Berry. Further hearings in West Germany were staged at the Benedictine Abbey in Ottobeuren in September 1964 and, two months later, at Münster – another city to have suffered the destruction of its ancient cathedral in a bombing raid during the Second World War. The first performance in East Germany was held at the Martin Luther Church in Dresden on 13 February 1965 and given by the Dresden Staatskapelle under Kurt Sanderling: the concert, scheduled to coincide with the emotive anniversary of the almost total destruction of the historic city by Allied bombing raids twenty years before, was immediately repeated on the following day. Japanese audiences heard the *War Requiem* for the first time eight days later when David Willcocks directed a performance at Tokyo's Metropolitan Festival Hall with 'the best talent available locally': the press noted that the work was already well known in the country through the wide dissemination of Britten's recording, which had been broadcast several times on local radio stations.[10]

Students from the Leningrad Conservatory presented Britten with a performance of an incomplete torso of the work during his visit to the Soviet Union later in the same year, 'at a time when the work was virtually forbidden in Russia'.[11] The first complete Russian performance took place on 23 May 1966. Meanwhile, the work had been heard several times in the United States, having been given in Boston and Connecticut in 1963. After its West Coast première at Larkspur on 6 December 1964, the reviewer for the *San Francisco Chronicle* wrote: 'Virtually any performance of the *War Requiem* would be a moving experience... It is a better than even chance that most of the two or three thousand listeners who packed Redwood Auditorium to the rafters will demand a second hearing. I can think of no better idea under the sun. Except possibly to form an international committee to present this work in every language, in every country in the world.'[12] Almost alone in failing to respond with unanimous sympathy was the city of Vienna, where the work was given on 24 October 1964 by the Vienna Philharmonic under Britten and Istvan Kertesz. When quizzed by the *London Magazine* in October 1963 about the Viennese reaction to the recording of the work, the composer had replied:

I have heard tell of a bad notice in Vienna, but I don't keep track of these things. It doesn't surprise me, as Vienna has always been *traditional* in its tastes, and the *War Requiem* is certainly not in the *traditional* 'avant-garde' language [of the Second Viennese School, i.e. Schoenberg, Berg and Webern]. But new works can be misunderstood not only for how they say something, but for *what* they say.

The composer did not amplify his final sentence, although its implied criticism of Vienna's failure to respond to the work's pacifist message is clear enough.

Throughout the performance history of the *War Requiem*, Peter Pears won consistent acclaim for his interpretation of the solo tenor part. At the Albert Hall in 1963 he achieved 'the perfect smoothness and remote quality ... that made the "Agnus Dei" one of the work's great moments'; nine years later he was praised for 'surpassing himself in beauty of line, warmth of tone, clarity of words and compassionate feeling'.[13] On 15 August 1976, less than four months before the composer's death, Pears appeared at the Albert Hall under Bernard Haitink in a live radio and television broadcast from the Proms, just one of nine performances of the work (two in Bavaria) undertaken by the 66-year-old tenor in that year alone. In May 1978, he was again to sing the work in Germany.

Two factors combined to help the *War Requiem* become a victim of its own success after the heady atmosphere surrounding its early performances began to abate. The first arose from increasing discomfort at the freedom with which the work had almost universally been accorded the label 'masterpiece' (a problem foreseen by Peter Evans in 1964), and the tone of some negative responses smacked sharply of sour grapes. William Mann's willingness to bestow this accolade even prior to the first performance had hardly helped, and doubtless fuelled the fires of those critics who had been hostile to Britten earlier in his career and who resented what they saw as his increasingly privileged position in British musical circles. These tensions had already exploded after the notorious gala première of *Gloriana* in 1953, but had been in evidence still earlier at around the time of the first performances of *Billy Budd* in 1951. As Stephen Williams was honest enough to admit,

One always resents having it dinned into one's ears that a new work is a masterpiece before it has been performed; and Benjamin Britten's *Billy Budd* was trumpeted into the arena by such a deafening roar of advance publicity that many of us entered

Covent Garden on Saturday (when the composer conducted the first performance) with a mean, sneaking hope that we might be able to flesh our fangs in it.[14]

As it happened, Williams was unable to 'flesh his fangs' on *Billy Budd* and ended his review by himself declaring the opera to be a masterpiece. But his revealing comments go far towards explaining why certain critical voices dissented from the generally perceived view of the *War Requiem* more than ten years later.

A major figure who deeply distrusted the extravagant welcome accorded the *War Requiem* in the early 1960s was Stravinsky, whose published comments on Britten show him to have been unaccountably sceptical of the younger composer's success. Stravinsky's remarks may appear uncharitable, but they have often been selectively quoted to give the impression that he was critical of Britten's music. In fact, his comments were strictly confined to discussing what would today doubtless be termed the 'hype' surrounding the early performances of the *War Requiem*:

The *War Requiem* is surely one of Britain's finest hours-and-a-half, yet the reception accorded the music was a phenomenon as remarkable as the music itself. In fact the Battle-of-Britten sentiment was so thick and the tide of applause so loud that I, for one, was not always able to hear the music. Behold *The Times*, in actual, Churchillian quotes: 'Few recordings can ever have been awaited so eagerly and by so many people ... practically everyone who has heard it has instantly acknowledged it as a masterpiece...' Farther along, after a stirring description of the 'grief-laden unison melody of the opening' and of the 'doom-laden funeral march', the same reviewer remarks that 'the grandeur and intensity of [Galina Vishnevskaya's] phrasing exorcize all conventional notions of angelic insipidness', meaning, I take it, that unconventional notions have the field. (In fact, Mme. V.'s singing is singularly harsh and out of tune.) ...

Kleenex at the ready, then, one goes from the critics to the music, knowing that if one should dare to disagree with 'practically everyone', one will be made to feel as if one had failed to stand up for '*God Save the Queen*'. The victim of all this, however, is the composer, for of course nothing fails like success, or hurts more than the press's ready certification of a 'masterpiece'.[15]

Stravinsky's implied condemnation of epithets such as 'grief-laden' and 'doom-laden' is not surprising from a composer who once controversially declared that 'music is essentially powerless to express anything at all', but he was by no means the only commentator to take Vishnevskaya's idiosyncratic reading of the solo soprano part to task. Another reviewer wrote of her 'difficulty in the accurate pitching of unfamiliar intervals and a certain rhythmic slackness [which] prevented the full characterisation of her music'.[16] Many felt Heather Harper's fine interpretation (both at the première and at numerous subsequent performances) to be definitive, and regretted the need for her to yield to Vishnevskaya when the latter was finally allowed by the Soviet authorities to participate.

The second problem concerns a very real inability on the part of listeners and critics alike to divorce the music of the *War Requiem* from its powerful subject-matter: how can the quality of the score be judged objectively when the gut reaction to its message is often one of emotional turmoil?[17] The atmosphere at the first performance was by all accounts so electric that objectivity was impossible. An illustration of the ease with which attitudes could be conditioned by this highly charged atmosphere was provided by Richard Butt of the BBC, who produced the live radio broadcast of the première. Butt recalled that when attempts to seat the long queue of attendees in the cathedral caused the performance to start late (Britten having insisted that it could not commence until everyone in the audience was settled), the radio announcer found himself with insufficient commentary to cover the resulting hiatus. Butt later received a number of letters from members of the public thanking him for 'that wonderful pause' before the performance.[18]

Desmond Shawe-Taylor alluded to this problem in January 1963:

Not for a long while can I hope to write of Benjamin Britten's *War Requiem* with the detachment that is supposed to be proper to criticism: the experience is still too immediate and overwhelming. If the work has its faults, I cannot yet see them. In more fertile centuries when masterpieces came thick and fast, the listener could perhaps absorb them with greater equanimity and less surprise. But this large, beautiful and profoundly original treatment of the central subject of our distracted age has arrived at a time of artistic scarcity, when the very notion of the masterpiece has even been scouted as so much obsolete romanticism; and its emotional impact is correspondingly great.[19]

Joan Chissell later noted that a 'first experience of a work as emotive as Britten's *War Requiem* can be overwhelming enough to induce a later reaction: there comes a moment when you may wonder whether it is the message rather than the actual music that moves'.[20] (She nevertheless added that 'all doubts on that score were quashed by Bernard Haitink's superbly committed performance' at the Festival Hall in January 1972.)

The impossibility of separating music and message has been exacerbated by the frequency with which the *War Requiem* has continued to be performed in emotive circumstances: the Coventry première and 1965 Dresden performance were not the only hearings to acquire special poignancy by direct association with an anniversary or momentous world event. On 1 September 1968, the work was performed at the Edinburgh Festival in the shadow of the Soviet invasion of Czechoslovakia. When the London Symphony Chorus took the *War Requiem* on an international tour as recently as 1991, a succession of coincidences lent added significance to the central theme of reconciliation between friend and foe. A pre-tour performance at London's Barbican Centre coincided with the eve of the land battle to liberate Kuwait from Iraqi troops during the Gulf War ('the tension among ... performers and audience was palpable'). A subsequent performance in Jerusalem by the Israel Philharmonic under Gary Bertini was arranged to commemorate the ceasefire in May, on which occasion chorus members were told of an Israeli soldier who had wept at an earlier performance of the work: 'until he heard Owen's words to Britten's music he had been unable to share his experience with anyone'. Also in May, a performance of the *War Requiem* at the historic Odeon of Herodes Atticus in Athens marked the fiftieth anniversary of the invasion of Crete by Nazi forces.[21]

In spite of an incipient malaise, few of the work's detractors were able to unearth specific defects in the score as evidence for their unease. Michael Kennedy reported that some listeners were disenchanted with what they saw as the 'sentimentality' of the work's closing pages 'and the perceived imbalance between the musical invention in the Requiem sections and the settings of the ... Owen war poems'. Following the growing fashion in the 1980s for dragging Britten's private life into the public arena at every opportunity, Kennedy went on to draw attention to Owen's oft-alleged homosexuality and declared that 'an unidentified revulsion from, or fear of, the sexual undertones in the work may account for its being disliked by some listeners'.[22]

We saw in Chapter 3, however, that the two musical 'flaws' cited by Kennedy – the 'sweetness' of the closing pages and the 'imbalance' between the Latin and Owen sections – are in fact elements contributing significantly to the score's ironic impact. Kennedy himself admitted as much when he wrote at greater length on the question of the need for detachment in assessing the work's artistic merit:

No one who was in Coventry Cathedral at the first performance will ever hear it with that 'objectivity' available to a later generation. But if the *War Requiem* was praised extravagantly at first, the reaction which set in later went too far the other way. If one looks at it dispassionately – which is how one could never *listen* to it – there is a disparity in invention between the large-scale liturgical sections and the Owen settings. The resemblances ... to Verdi's *Requiem* (and also, I think, to Mahler's *Resurrection* Symphony) in the *Dies Irae* are disturbing, the orchestral writing much more obvious and conventional. Yet it seems likely that this was deliberate on Britten's part in order to highlight the instrumental detail in the Owen poems (and his scoring of these for the chamber orchestra is at his highest level). It is not surprising that the Owen settings are the finest and most characteristic music, for Britten is at his best in dealing with the dark and secret places of the heart, with the private rather than the public.[23]

The Verdi 'flaw' had also been spotted by Peter Heyworth at the time of the first performance, and he went on to conclude that 'as the work moves to its end ... Britten draws a great veil of consolation over so much suffering and sacrifice.'[24] This was an early example of the ease with which a listener could be led (presumably by the 'sentimentality' and 'sweetness' discussed by Kennedy) into regarding the ending of the work as comforting. As we have suggested (p. 77), the score ends with a disconcerting gesture which appears to deflate the consolatory effect of the tranquil 'Let us sleep now ...', and forces us to regard the foregoing musical reconciliation of all the participating forces with more than a hint of scepticism.

A similar lack of receptivity to the work's complex ironies was demonstrated by Peter Shaffer at the time of the première, when he declared that 'almost alone among contemporary works of music, it offers *true consolation*' (my italics: 'true compassion' might have been a more accurate phrase).[25] More seriously, Shaffer was strangely impervious to the often scathing indictment of liturgical platitudes promoted by Britten's strategic placement of the Owen texts: he concluded that the work's message was 'war is blasphemy', implying that conventional religious beliefs emerge unscathed from the textual juxtapositions. Peter Stadlen threw up his hands in horror in 1964 at the suggestion by a *Daily Telegraph* reader that Britten's attitude towards Christianity might be open to question:

What right did I have, asked my correspondent, to assume Britten's adherence to the Christian faith? Given the churches' refusal to denounce war unconditionally, no one, he claimed, who 'labours under the misapprehension that the *War Requiem* springs from religious convictions' could fully comprehend 'this tremendous affirmation of faith in mankind'...

It is touching (and it unexpectedly adds to one's list of don'ts) to find that the dyed-in-the-wool atheist can be as sensitive as the believer and, of course, it just goes to show how universal is the appeal of that unique work.

However, we need not ponder too seriously whether the confrontation of the Requiem text with Owen's war poems was done in a spirit of irony and sacrilege (as would be the case if my correspondent were right)... this [is] hardly to be expected of a composer who turns so frequently to sacred subjects.[26]

Stadlen was not, of course, aware at the time of Britten's disbelief in the divinity of Christ (cf. p. 16), but his short-sightedness in so complacently dismissing the most important level of irony in the *War Requiem* is extraordinary. Yet these misapprehensions have continued to flourish, and as recently as 1992 Edward Rothstein fell prey to both booby traps when he deemed the liturgical sections of the score to be more satisfying than the Owen settings:

The Latin choral sections, the most affecting musical episodes, are almost always sarcastically undercut, sometimes by orchestral accompaniments, generally by the interpolations of thematically related poems. The musical juxtapositions may be sophisticated in their design but are as blunt in their intentions as Owen's texts. Great music of mourning can expand both sorrow and understanding as it proceeds; this Requiem seems to contract, conflating distinctions into a single sentiment.

... There is a fallacy at the heart of this work, that depletes it of tragedy and intricacy and makes its reconciliation seem too easily won. The musical result, at any rate, is still worth hearing on Memorial Day, when we are meant to mourn those fallen in battle, though unlike Britten, we might admit some of those battles to have been necessary.[27]

The assertion that the work's 'reconciliation' seems 'easily won' would seem surprising, were it not for the obvious (and, nearly fifty years after the Second World War, scarcely credible) prejudice against conscientious objectors displayed in the final sentence: yet one further illustration of the manifold difficulties encountered in attempting any objective assessment of the *War Requiem*.

Kennedy's remark that 'Britten is at his best in dealing with the dark and secret places of the heart, with the private rather than the public' reminds us that the *War Requiem* may ultimately be concerned with the same intense dichotomy between private anxiety and public responsibility which surfaces with such force in certain of Britten's operas, notably *Billy Budd*, *Gloriana*, *The Turn of the Screw* and *Death in Venice*. It is, after all, a comparable moral dichotomy which affects the non-combatant in times of war: as Britten himself observed of his own wartime experiences, 'As conscientious objectors we were out of it. We couldn't say we suffered physically, but naturally we experienced tremendous tension' (see p. 17). Some commentators have found the comparable public–private tension in the *War Requiem* disconcerting, Robin Holloway writing in 1977 that 'the "public" manner of the

War Requiem [seemed] a betrayal of the authentic voice of the *Serenade*, the *Nocturne*, the *Winter Words*'.[28] Yet it is a fundamental and inescapable element of the ambiguities and tensions expressed equally vividly elsewhere in Britten's output.

Since Britten's death in 1976, the stature of the *War Requiem* has continued to grow. The long monopoly enjoyed by the composer's recorded interpretation of the work was broken in February 1983 by the making of a new recording by Simon Rattle with the City of Birmingham Symphony Orchestra, the orchestra which had played at the Coventry première twenty-one years before. When Rattle conducted the work at the Royal Opera House in 1986 at a memorial concert for Pears, his interpretation was hailed as 'highly theatrical... Indeed, in these surroundings, the work sounded more like an extension of Britten's operas than an oratorio.'[29] This parallel recalls the precedent of Verdi's Requiem, to which Britten's score owes so much; it also brings to mind William Plomer's assertion that the theme of innocence versus experience which is so frequently explored in Britten's stage works is also echoed in the *War Requiem*.[30] Two further interpretations were recorded in the early 1990s, the first under the direction of Richard Hickox (1991) and the second a live recording by John Eliot Gardiner (1993). In a further parallel with Britten's operas, which some gloomy critics felt might prove to be inseparable from their original interpreters, a new generation of performers was strengthening the work's assured future in the concert hall and record catalogues. Among the more notable readings to have emerged since the composer's death have been those by Mstislav Rostropovich (Vishnevskaya's husband) and the intensely dramatic interpretation by Kurt Masur.

The *War Requiem* had shown itself to be commercially as well as artistically viable with the astonishing success of Britten's 1963 recording. In 1988 the British director Derek Jarman produced a controversial film interpretation with the composer's complete recording as its soundtrack, and immediately laid himself open to charges of exploiting the work's mass appeal for his own ends. When granting Jarman permission to use the recording, Decca stipulated that no sound effects or spoken text would be heard simultaneously with the music; but commercial interests seemed not far below the surface when it was noted that the film's release coincided with the recording company's promotion of the relatively new medium of CD video.[31] Jarman's *War Requiem* was shot entirely on location at Darenth Park Hospital (a disused mental institution near Dartford), with the trench scenes enacted in the boiler room and Laurence Olivier appearing as an old soldier to recite 'Strange Meeting' by way of prologue. Jarman declared of the project: 'I do feel a bit nervous... Owen took on the war; Britten took on Owen and the Mass; I'm taking on all three.'[32] Critical reaction to the film was mixed, few reviewers finding the result as satisfying as Jarman might have wished. Nigella Lawson pointed out that Owen's attempt to portray the horrors of war in all their stark reality was scarcely in tune with the 'beautiful' and symbolic visual images conjured up by the director.[33] David Robinson, diplomatically echoing the sentiments of many who found the addition of visual interest to Britten's score entirely pointless, commented that 'Britten's music ... inevitably dwarfs anything set beside it' and complained that Jarman's scenes sometimes 'seem small and banal beside the aural impression'.[34] Only in the 'Libera me', where genuine archival war footage (from the bloody Cambodian conflict) accompanied the build-up to the cataclysmic climax on the G minor chord at Fig. 116 (the nuclear attack on Hiroshima), did the film seem convincingly in harmony with the music. Jarman was predictably defensive:

I have no sympathy whatsoever for purists who say 'How dare you use classical music!' The nature of the music is changed irrevocably by the act of recording it, but nobody complains about that anymore...

So I would have been absolutely horrified if they [i.e. Britten's Trustees] hadn't let me do it. How would they be able to justify themselves, since Britten also had to get permission from the Owen estate to use his poems? We are not making an attempt to supersede Britten's work. To destroy the *War Requiem*, to make it completely unlistenable, would require a feat of brilliance![35]

Alongside high-level performances, recordings and other commercial ventures, the *War Requiem* has continued to astonish by securing for itself a permanent niche in the ever more ambitious repertoire tackled by amateur choral societies and university music clubs. As early as 1964, the choir and orchestra of the Cambridge University Musical Society performed the score under the joint direction of the composer and David Willcocks, first in King's College Chapel on 9 June and again on the following day in Ely Cathedral as part of the seventeenth Aldeburgh Festival. Here, perhaps, can be seen the truth of Colin Mason's assertion that the piece is 'almost certainly the most important work in the history of English choral music since [Elgar's *Dream of*] *Gerontius*, and a reminder that Britten has not only brought about a rebirth of English opera but has contributed perhaps more vitally than any of his contemporaries, even those who have concentrated on choral music, to the continuance of the so-called "English choral tradition"'.[36] It is one of the richest ironies of the *War Requiem*'s performance history that a work embodying fundamentally anti-establishment sentiments, attacking both the inhumanity of war and the complacency of conventional religion, should have become one of the most enduring bastions of the British musical establishment.

'Every performance it is given ought to be a momentous occasion', wrote William Mann in 1962. Over the decades since, in whichever corner of the globe, whether performed by amateurs or professionals, whether in emotive or neutral circumstances, Mann's prognosis for the *War Requiem* has proved to be unnervingly accurate. There may ultimately be no simple answers to the disturbing social and artistic questions which this singular work poses, but – as is so often the case in Britten operas – it is this very fact which has secured the *War Requiem* a consistently thought-provoking position at the centre of the select canon of twentieth-century choral masterpieces.

Appendix. Text

I Requiem aeternam

CHORUS

Requiem aeternam dona eis Domine,   Rest eternal grant them, Lord;
et lux perpetua luceat eis.   and may everlasting light shine upon them.

BOYS' CHOIR

Te decet hymnus, Deus in Sion;   Songs of praise are due to Thee, God, in Zion;
et tibi reddetur votum in Jerusalem;   and prayers offered up to Thee in Jerusalem;
exaudi orationem meam,   hear my prayer,
ad te omnis caro veniet.   all flesh shall come to Thee.

TENOR SOLO

What passing-bells for these who die as cattle?
   Only the monstrous anger of the guns.
   Only the stuttering rifles' rapid rattle
Can patter out their hasty orisons.
No mockeries for them from prayers or bells,
   Nor any voice of mourning save the choirs, –
The shrill, demented choirs of wailing shells;
   And bugles calling for them from sad shires.

What candles may be held to speed them all?
   Not in the hands of boys, but in their eyes
Shall shine the holy glimmers of good-byes.
   The pallor of girls' brows shall be their pall;
Their flowers the tenderness of silent minds,
And each slow dusk a drawing-down of blinds.
                 ['Anthem for Doomed Youth']

CHORUS

Kyrie eleison,   Lord have mercy,
Christe eleison,   Christ have mercy,
Kyrie eleison.   Lord have mercy.

II Dies irae

Day of wrath, day of morning [handwritten]

CHORUS

Dies irae, dies illa,
Solvet saeclum in favilla,
Teste David cum Sibylla.

Day of anger, that day,
Shall dissolve this generation into ashes,
With David and the Sibyl as witness.

Quantus tremor est futurus,
Quando Judex est venturus,
Cuncta stricte discussurus!

How much quaking there will be,
When the Judge will come,
To weigh all things strictly.

Tuba mirum spargens sonum
Per sepulchra regionum
Coget omnes ante thronum.

The trumpet pouring forth its awful sound
Through the tombs of the lands
Drives everyone before the throne.

Mors stupebit et natura,
Cum resurget creatura,
Judicanti responsura.

Death shall be stunned, and nature,
When life shall rise again,
To answer for itself before the Judge.

BARITONE SOLO

Bugles sang, saddening the evening air,
And bugles answered, sorrowful to hear.

Voices of boys were by the river-side.
Sleep mothered them; and left the twilight sad.
The shadow of the morrow weighed on men.

Voices of old despondency resigned,
Bowed by the shadow of the morrow, slept.

[untitled]

SOPRANO SOLO AND CHORUS

Liber scriptus proferetur,
In quo totum continetur,
Unde mundus judicetur.

A book inscribed shall be brought forth,
In which all is contained,
From which the world shall be judged.

Judex ergo cum sedebit,
Quidquid latet, apparebit:
Nil inultum remanebit.

When the Judge, therefore, shall sit,
Whatever is concealed shall appear:
Nothing unavenged shall remain.

Quid sum miser tunc dicturus?
Quem patronum rogaturus,
Cum vix justus sit securus?

What am I, a wretch, to say then?
To whom as defender shall I entreat,
Since the just man is scarcely safe?

Rex tremendae majestatis,	King of fearful majesty,
Qui salvandos salvas gratis,	Who freely savest those who are to be saved,
Salva me, fons pietatis.	Save me, fountain of compassion.

TENOR AND BARITONE SOLOS

Out there, we've walked quite friendly up to Death;
   Sat down and eaten with him, cool and bland, –
Pardoned his spilling mess-tins in our hand.
We've sniffed the green thick odour of his breath, –
Our eyes wept, but our courage didn't writhe.
He's spat at us with bullets and he's coughed
   Shrapnel. We chorussed when he sang aloft;
We whistled while he shaved us with his scythe.

Oh, Death was never enemy of ours!
   We laughed at him, we leagued with him, old chum.
No soldier's paid to kick against his powers.
   We laughed, knowing that better men would come,
And greater wars; when each proud fighter brags
He wars on Death – for life; not men – for flags.

               ['The Next War']

CHORUS

Recordare Jesu pie,	Recall, kind Jesus,
Quod sum causa tuae viae:	That I am the reason for your being:
Ne me perdas illa die.	Lest Thou do away with me on that day.
Quaerens me, sedisti lassus:	Searching for me, Thou didst sit exhausted:
Redemisti crucem passus:	Thou hast redeemed me by suffering the cross:
Tantus labor non sit cassus.	So much toil should not be in vain.
Ingemisco, tamquam reus:	I sigh, so great a sinner:
Culpa rubet vultus meus:	Guilt reddens my face:
Supplicanti parce Deus.	Spare the supplicant, God.
Qui Mariam absolvisti,	Thou who hast forgiven Mary,
Et latronem exaudisti,	And hast listened to the robber,
Mihi quoque spem dedisti.	And hast also given hope to me.
Inter oves locum praesta,	Set me down amongst the sheep,
Et ab haedis me sequestra,	And remove me from the goats,
Statuens in parte dextra.	Standing at Thy right hand.

Confutatis maledictis,	With the damned confounded,
Flammis acribus addictis,	To the crackling flames consigned,
Voca me cum benedictis.	Call me with your saints.
Oro supplex et acclinis,	I pray, kneeling and suppliant,
Cor contritum quasi cinis:	My heart worn away like ashes:
Gere curam mei finis.	Protect me at my ending.

BARITONE SOLO

Be slowly lifted up, thou long black arm,
Great gun towering toward Heaven, about to curse;

Reach at that arrogance which needs thy harm,
And beat it down before its sins grow worse;

But when thy spell be cast complete and whole,
May God curse thee, and cut thee from our soul!
[from 'Sonnet: On Seeing a Piece of Our Artillery Brought into Action']

CHORUS AND SOPRANO SOLO

Dies irae, dies illa,	Day of anger, that day,
Solvet saeclum in favilla,	Shall dissolve this generation into ashes,
Teste David cum Sibylla.	With David and the Sibyl as witness.
Quantus tremor est futurus,	How much quaking there will be,
Quando judex est venturus,	When the Judge will come,
Cuncta stricte discussurus!	To weigh all things strictly.
Lacrimosa dies illa,	That tearful day,
Qua resurget ex favilla,	On which shall arise again from the ashes,
Judicandus homo reus,	The sinner to be judged,
Huic ergo parce Deus.	Spare him accordingly, God.

TENOR SOLO

Move him into the sun –
Gently its touch awoke him once,
At home, whispering of fields unsown.
Always it woke him, even in France,
Until this morning and this snow.
If anything might rouse him now
The kind old sun will know.

Think how it wakes the seeds, –
Woke, once, the clays of a cold star.
Are limbs, so dear-achieved, are sides,
Full-nerved – still warm – too hard to stir?
Was it for this the clay grew tall?
– O what made fatuous sunbeams toil
To break earth's sleep at all?

['Futility']

CHORUS

Pie Jesu Domine,   Kind Jesus, Lord,
dona eis requiem.   grant them rest.
Amen.   Amen.

III Offertorium

BOYS' CHOIR

Domine Jesu Christe,   Lord Jesus Christ,
Rex gloriae,   King of glory,
libera animas omnium fidelium   free the souls of all the faithful
defunctorum de poenis inferni,   dead from the tortures of hell,
et de profondo lacu: and from the bottomless pit:
libera eas de ore leonis,   free them from the mouth of the lion,
ne absorbeat eas tartarus,   that hell may not swallow them up,
ne cadant in obscurum.   nor may they fall into darkness.

CHORUS

Sed signifer sanctus Michael   But the holy standard-bearer Michael
repraesentet eas in lucem sanctam: shall bring them back into the holy light:
quam olim Abrahae promisisti,   as Thou once didst promise to Abraham,
et semini ejus.   and his offspring.

BARITONE AND TENOR SOLOS

So Abram rose, and clave the wood, and went,
And took the fire with him, and a knife.
And as they sojourned both of them together,
Isaac the first-born spake and said, My Father,
Behold the preparations, fire and iron,
But where the lamb for this burnt-offering?
Then Abram bound the youth with belts and straps,
And builded parapets and trenches there,

96

And stretchèd forth the knife to slay his son.
When lo! an angel called him out of heaven,
Saying, Lay not thy hand upon the lad,
Neither do anything to him. Behold,
A ram, caught in a thicket by its horns;
Offer the Ram of Pride instead of him.
But the old man would not so, but slew his son, –
And half the seed of Europe, one by one.
      ['The Parable of the Old Man and the Young']

BOYS' CHOIR

Hostias et preces	Sacrifices and prayers
tibi Domine laudis offerimus:	we offer to Thee, Lord, with praise:
tu suscipe pro animabus illis,	receive them for the souls of those
quarum hodie memoriam facimus:	whose memory we recall today:
fac eas, Domine,	make them, Lord,
de morte transire ad vitam.	to pass from death to life.

IV Sanctus

SOPRANO SOLO AND CHORUS

Sanctus, sanctus, sanctus	Holy, holy, holy
Dominus Deus Sabaoth.	Lord God of Hosts.
Pleni sunt coeli et terra gloria tua,	Full are heaven and earth with Thy glory.
Hosanna in excelsis.	Hosanna in the highest.

Benedictus qui venit in nomine Domini.	Blessed is he who comes in the name of the Lord.
Hosanna in excelsis.	Hosanna in the highest.

BARITONE SOLO

After the blast of lightning from the East,
The flourish of loud clouds, the Chariot Throne;
After the drums of Time have rolled and ceased,
And by the bronze west long retreat is blown,

Shall life renew these bodies? Of a truth
All death will He annul, all tears assuage? –
Fill the void veins of Life again with youth,
And wash, with an immortal water, Age?

When I do ask white Age he saith not so:
'My head hangs weighed with snow.'
And when I hearken to the Earth, she saith:
'My fiery heart shrinks, aching. It is death.
Mine ancient scars shall not be glorified,
Nor my titanic tears, the sea, be dried.'

['The End']

V Agnus Dei

TENOR SOLO

One ever hangs where shelled roads part.
    In this war He too lost a limb,
But His disciples hide apart;
    And now the Soldiers bear with Him.

CHORUS

Agnus Dei,   Lamb of God,
qui tollis peccata mundi,   who takest away the sins of the world,
dona eis requiem.   grant them rest.

TENOR SOLO

Near Golgotha strolls many a priest,
    And in their faces there is pride
That they were flesh-marked by the Beast
    By whom the gentle Christ's denied.

CHORUS

Agnus Dei,   Lamb of God,
qui tollis peccata mundi,   who takest away the sins of the world,
dona eis requiem.   grant them rest.

TENOR SOLO

The scribes on all the people shove
And bawl allegiance to the state,
But they who love the greater love
Lay down their life; they do not hate.

['At a Calvary near the Ancre']

CHORUS

Agnus Dei,   Lamb of God,
qui tollis peccata mundi,   who takest away the sins of the world,
dona eis requiem sempiternam.   grant them rest everlasting.

TENOR SOLO
Dona nobis pacem.   Grant us peace.

VI Libera me

CHORUS AND SOPRANO SOLO

Libera me, Domine, de morte aeterna,	Free me, Lord, from eternal death,
in die illa tremenda:	on that dreadful day.
Quando coeli movendi sunt et terra:	When the skies and ground shall quake:
Dum veneris judicare	When Thou comest to judge
saeculum per ignem.	our generation through fire.
Tremens factus sum ego, et timeo,	I am made to tremble, and am afraid,
dum discussio venerit,	until the trial shall come,
atque ventura ira.	and the anger arrive.
Libera me, Domine, de morte aeterna,	Free me, Lord, from eternal death,
Quando coeli movendi sunt et terra.	When the skies and ground shall quake.
Dies illa, dies irae,	That day, day of anger,
calamitatis et miseriae,	of disaster and misery,
dies magna et amara valde.	a great day and intensely bitter.
Libera me, Domine ...	Free me, Lord ...

TENOR SOLO

It seemed that out of battle I escaped
Down some profound dull tunnel, long since scooped
Through granites which titanic wars had groined.
Yet also there encumbered sleepers groaned,
Too fast in thought or death to be bestirred.
Then, as I probed them, one sprang up, and stared
With piteous recognition in fixed eyes,
Lifting distressful hands as if to bless.
And no guns thumped, or down the flues made moan.
'Strange friend,' I said, 'here is no cause to mourn.'

BARITONE SOLO

'None,' said the other, 'save the undone years,
The hopelessness. Whatever hope is yours,
Was my life also; I went hunting wild
After the wildest beauty in the world.

For by my glee might many men have laughed,
And of my weeping something had been left,
Which must die now. I mean the truth untold,

The pity of war, the pity war distilled.
Now men will go content with what we spoiled.
Or, discontent, boil bloody, and be spilled.
They will be swift with swiftness of the tigress,
None will break ranks, though nations trek from progress.
Miss we the march of this retreating world
Into vain citadels that are not walled.
Then, when much blood had clogged their chariot-wheels,
I would go up and wash them from sweet wells,
Even from wells we sunk too deep for war,
Even the sweetest wells that ever were.

I am the enemy you killed, my friend.
I knew you in this dark; for so you frowned
Yesterday through me as you jabbed and killed.
I parried; but my hands were loath and cold.'

TENOR AND BARITONE SOLOS
'Let us sleep now ... '
['Strange Meeting']

BOYS' CHOIR, CHORUS AND SOPRANO SOLO

In paradisum deducant te Angeli:	To heaven may the Angels escort you:
in tuo adventu suscipiant te Martyres,	on your arrival may the Martyrs accept you,
et perducant te	and lead you
in civitatem sanctam Jerusalem.	to the sacred city Jerusalem.
Chorus Angelorum te suscipiat,	May the Choir of Angels receive you,
et cum Lazaro quondam paupere	and with Lazarus, once a pauper,
aeternam habeas requiem.	may you have rest eternal.
Requiem aeternam dona eis, Domine;	Rest eternal grant them, Lord,
et lux perpetua luceat eis.	and may everlasting light shine upon them.
Requiescant in pace.	May they rest in peace.
Amen.	Amen.

Notes

1 Owen, Britten and pacifism

1 The most important source for information on Wilfred Owen's childhood and early development is Harold Owen's memoirs, published in three volumes under the collective title *Journey from obscurity* (London, 1963–5). The work is more conveniently available as a single-volume abridgement prepared by Hilary M. Gornall (Oxford, 1968).

2 *Wilfred Owen: selected letters*, ed. J. Bell, p. 71.

3 Letter dated 4 April 1915; ibid., p. 147.

4 Letter dated 10 August 1914; ibid., p. 111.

5 See Stallworthy, *Wilfred Owen: a biography*, pp. 104–5. The closing lines of 'Dulce et Decorum Est' are quoted at the head of the present volume.

6 Letter dated 6 November 1914; *Selected letters*, p. 128.

7 Strachey's appearance before a conscientious-objection tribunal was humorously described by Robert Graves: 'Asked by the chairman the usual question: "I understand, Mr Strachey, that you have a conscientious objection to war?", he replied (in his curious falsetto voice), "Oh, no, not at all, only to *this* war." And to the chairman's other stock question, which had previously never failed to embarrass the claimant: "Tell me, Mr Strachey, what would you do if you saw a German soldier trying to violate your sister?" he replied with an air of noble virtue: "I would try to get between them." ' (*Goodbye to all that*, p. 205.) Strachey's pacifist stance was especially notable because he was in any case medically unfit for service. Britten's (perhaps not coincidental) interest in his work was revealed in 1952 when he based his coronation opera *Gloriana* on Strachey's 1928 novel *Elizabeth and Essex*.

8 *Selected letters*, p. 128.

9 Letter dated 2 December 1914; ibid., p. 130. The emphasis is Owen's.

10 Undated postcard from Owen to his mother; ibid., p. 157.

11 Undated letter, *c.* June 1915; ibid., p. 153. The emphasis is Owen's.

12 It was from Keats that Owen inherited his fondness for fourteen-line sonnet form: of the nine Owen poems selected by Britten for inclusion in the *War Requiem*, no fewer than five are sonnets.

13 In a letter to his mother written on 5 March 1916, Owen related that Monro was ' "very struck" with [my] sonnets. He went over the things in detail and he told me what was fresh and clever, and what was second-hand and banal; and what Keatsian and what "modern" ' (*Selected letters*, p. 181).

14 For Shelley's influence on 'Strange Meeting', see Stallworthy, *Wilfred Owen*, p. 256. Pararhyme is a form of rhyme (ponderously termed 'consonantal end-rhyme' by C. Day Lewis in his edition of *The collected poems of Wilfred Owen*, p. 25) in which the vowel sound is modified but the consonants remain constant. 'Strange Meeting' is entirely written in pararhymed couplets:

> It seemed that out of battle I escaped
> Down some profound dull tunnel, long since scooped
> Through granites which titanic wars had groined.
> Yet also there encumbered sleepers groaned . . .

See Stallworthy, *Wilfred Owen*, pp. 70 and 105–6, for further comment on Owen's development of the technique.

15 Graves, *Goodbye to all that*, p. 146.

16 *Selected letters*, pp. 269–70.

17 Quoted in Stallworthy, *Wilfred Owen*, p. 206.

18 Letter from Ivor Gurney to Marion Scott, 29 September 1917; *Ivor Gurney: war letters*, ed. R. K. R. Thornton, p. 231.

19 For a firsthand account of Sassoon's activities at this time, see Graves, *Goodbye to all that*, pp. 211–28.

20 Letter dated 6 June 1917; *Selected letters*, p. 252.

21 Letter from Owen to his mother dated 2 October 1917; ibid., pp. 281–2.

22 Letter from Owen to his mother dated 25 September 1917; ibid., p. 280.

23 Undated letter (*c.* 16 May 1917), ibid., p. 246.

24 Letter dated 13 August 1917; ibid., p. 268. The closing remark is an adaptation of the famous quotation from Romans 12:19 used by Tolstoy as the motto for *Anna Karenina*.

25 Graves, *Goodbye to all that*, pp. 157–8. With Catholic chaplains, however, it was an altogether different story since they were constantly required to administer the rite of extreme unction in the midst of battle.

26 Letter to Marion Scott, 26 September 1917; *War letters*, p. 206.

27 Graves, *Goodbye to all that*, p. 157.

28 Letter to Marion Scott, 17 February 1917; *War letters*, p. 136.

29 See Hibberd, 'Concealed messages in Wilfred Owen's trench letters'.

30 Letters from Owen to his mother dated 23 July 1915 (*Selected letters*, p. 158) and 1 January 1917 (ibid., p. 207). Grisly trench humour was rife: Graves tells how the soldiers in his platoon would jocularly shake the stiffly outstretched hand of a nearby corpse with the words 'Put it there, Billy Boy' (*Goodbye to all that*, p. 97).

31 See *Selected letters*, pp. 237 and 243–4. Similarly, Graves and Gurney both collected souvenirs from the battlefield, the latter (who, unlike Graves and Owen, was a private soldier) commenting that 'only the officers have any real good chance of souvenirs, since only they can get them off'.

32 The complete text of the citation is quoted in Stallworthy, *Wilfred Owen*, p. 279 note 1. Hibberd (*Wilfred Owen: the last year*, p. 174) compares facsimiles of the two existing 'official' documents recording the citation, and fascinatingly concludes that one was a forgery concocted by Owen's parents along the lines of his letter of 4 October; it replaces the uncomfortable statement that their son 'inflicted considerable losses on the enemy' with a more acceptable phrase to the effect that he merely 'took a number of prisoners'.

33 Letter from Owen to his mother dated 4 October 1918; *Selected letters*, p. 351.

34 Only five poems by Owen were published during their author's lifetime. These were 'Song of Songs' and 'The Next War' (published anonymously in Owen's Craiglockhart journal *The Hydra*, 1 and 29 September 1917 respectively), 'Miners' (*The Nation*, 26 January 1918), 'Hospital Barge' and 'Futility' (both appearing in *The Nation*, 15 June 1918).

In 1919 Edith Sitwell published seven of Owen's poems (including 'Strange Meeting') in her annual anthology *Wheels*, and dedicated the issue to his memory. Then, thirteen months after Owen's death, Siegfried Sassoon and Edith Sitwell published an independent collection of twenty-three Owen poems (*Poems by Wilfred Owen*, with an Introduction by Sassoon, London, 1920; reprinted 1921). The first collected edition, edited by C. Day Lewis with a

Memoir by Edmund Blunden, appeared in 1963 and was based on an earlier incomplete edition by Blunden (1931).

35 C. Day Lewis, Introduction to *The collected poems*, p. 27.

36 *Guardian*, 7 June 1971.

37 Letter from Auden to Stephen Spender, 1941; quoted in John Evans, '*Owen Wingrave*: a case for pacifism' in C. Palmer (ed.), *The Britten companion*, p. 227.

38 For a full discussion of the background to the film, see D. Mitchell, *Britten and Auden in the thirties: the year 1936*, pp. 64–7.

39 A facsimile of the *Pacifist March*, as published by the PPU, is included in Mitchell, *Britten and Auden*, pp. 68–9. Other marches similar in idiom are to be found in Britten's *Russian Funeral* (1936) and Piano Concerto (1938).

40 Duncan, *Working with Britten*, p. 34. Duncan mistitles the book 'The Technique of Non-Violence'.

41 Mitchell, *Britten and Auden*, pp. 142–4.

42 Quoted in H. Carpenter, *Benjamin Britten: a biography*, p. 137.

43 Letter from Britten to Enid Slater, 7 November 1939; *Letters from a life: selected letters and diaries of Benjamin Britten 1913–76*, eds. D. Mitchell and P. Reed, p. 725.

44 Quoted in Carpenter, *Britten*, p. 146.

45 *Sunday Times*, 15 June 1941.

46 *Letters from a life*, pp. 1046–9.

47 For a facsimile of the certificate, see ibid., p. 1058.

48 Schafer, *British composers in interview*, pp. 116–17. See also P. Brett (ed.), *Benjamin Britten: 'Peter Grimes'*, pp. 187 and 190.

49 Quoted in Carpenter, *Britten*, p. 139.

50 M. Kennedy, *Britten*, p. 251.

51 *Pacifist* 15/3 (January 1977). Tippett's brief obituary of Britten was printed on the front cover of this issue of the Peace Pledge Union's official journal, with an extract from the vocal score of the *War Requiem* ('Anthem for Doomed Youth') as background.

2 The *War Requiem* in progress

1 For a complete account of the design and construction of the cathedral, see Basil Spence, *Phoenix at Coventry: the building of a cathedral* (London, 1962) and Louis Campbell, *Coventry Cathedral: art and architecture in post-war Britain* (Oxford, 1996). A contentious view of Spence's achievement at Coventry was contributed to the *Independent* (10 June 1992) by Peter Dormer, 'Aiming for the eternal and missing'.

2 Note at this stage the solution eventually adopted at the first performances – namely using two conductors, one for the chamber orchestra and another for the main orchestra and choir – had not occurred to Britten. See pp. 27–8.

3 See Donald Mitchell, 'Down there on a visit: a meeting with Christopher Isherwood, Santa Monica, 22 April 1978', *London Magazine* 32/12 (April/May 1992), pp. 80–7; reprinted in *Cradles of the new: writings on music 1951–91*, selected by C. Palmer, ed. M. Cooke, pp. 441–9.

4 Vishnevskaya, *Galina: a Russian story*, p. 365.

5 Pears offered a conflicting explanation to Michael Kennedy in 1986: '[Vishnevskaya] was in fact contracted to sing at the Bol'shoy in Moscow, in *Falstaff* actually – which was not a very big part for her. However, they wouldn't think of letting her off ... that was out of the question' (Michael Kennedy, 'The idea was good: a study of Britten's *War Requiem*', BBC Radio 3 (17 February 1986); transcript held at the Britten–Pears Library).

6 See Kathleen Mitchell, 'Edinburgh Diary 1968' in Reed (ed.), *On Mahler and Britten: essays in honour of Donald Mitchell on his 70th birthday*, pp. 206–7.

7 The programme, entitled 'Personal Choice', was broadcast by the BBC Home Service on 16 July 1958. Although Britten generally excluded poems he had already set to music – an

exception was Hardy's 'If it's ever Spring again' which he had set but then excluded from the song-cycle *Winter Words* – many of Britten's choices reflected his current compositional preoccupations, notably Shakespeare's 'When most I wink' (Sonnet 43) and an excerpt from Coleridge's 'The Wanderings of Cain', both of which found their way into the *Nocturne*, Op. 60. (He also chose Edith Sitwell's 'The Youth with Red-gold Hair', a poem which Britten thought of including in *Nocturne*: an unfinished sketch page survives.) For a complete list of Britten's selection, see White, *Benjamin Britten: his life and operas*, p. 88.

8 Stallworthy notes that 'Bugles sang' was written 'shortly before Wilfred Owen read the anonymous Prefatory Note to *Poems of Today: an Anthology* (1916), that triggered *Anthem for Doomed Youth*'. See Stallworthy (ed.), *The poems of Wilfred Owen*, p. 179.

9 *The poems of Wilfred Owen*, edited with a Memoir by Edmund Blunden (London, 1955), p. 179.

10 Ibid., p. 134.

11 Rosamund Strode (Britten's music assistant, 1963–76), who assisted Imogen Holst (the composer's previous assistant) in preparing the full score of the *War Requiem* for Britten, told the present writer (in 1994) that she always felt that Pears was rather closely involved in the selection of the Owen texts. No archival evidence has come to light to support this belief; however, we must recognize that the extent of Britten's and Pears's discussion of the project cannot be known.

In the prelims to the published vocal score, where the entire text of the work is carefully laid out (at Britten's insistence), the words 'Dona nobis pacem' appear in italics, a typographical indication that they do not belong to the words of the Latin Requiem Mass.

12 Fol. 70ᵛ contains a four-bar sketch of the vocal entries at Fig. 2 ('et lux perpetua'), showing Britten once again working out the use of overlapping vocal entries.

13 The orchestra's dotted motif from this setting is one of four brief sketches located in the final pages of Britten's 1961 pocket diary. Each sketch probably represents the first occasion on which any material for the work was written down. The other sketches are: the fugue subject, adapted from *Canticle II*, for 'Quam olim Abrahae promisisti et semini ejus' (in A major); the opening bar of the 'Lacrimosa'; and the first phrase of the plainsong 'In paradisum' from the closing pages of the 'Libera me'.

14 Imogen Holst added a cautionary note to the copyist of the 'Libera me': 'Please take *all* voice parts from vocal score, NOT from this score, where they are only roughly indicated.'

15 As Humphrey Carpenter points out (*Benjamin Britten*, p. 406), a programme note by William Mann that was used at several performances in the 1960s, many of which were conducted by Britten, incorrectly claims that the composer inscribed the *War Requiem* 'to the memory of four friends who died in the second world war'.

16 See Mitchell and Reed (eds.), *Letters from a life*, p. 1035.

17 See James Rusbridger, *Who sank Surcouf?: the truth about the disappearance of the pride of the French Navy* (London, 1991), pp. 104–7. The volume also includes a photograph of Burney.

18 Interview with John Pounder by Donald Mitchell and Philip Reed (24 June 1989), the Britten–Pears Library.

19 Britten to Pears, 9 April 1944: 'Isn't it tragic about Michael Halliday being missing. I feel very odd about it now – poor silly old dear that he was' (*Letters from a life*, p. 1192).

20 For fuller accounts of Dunkerley's relationship with Britten, see *Letters from a life*, pp. 401–8, and Carpenter, *Benjamin Britten*, pp. 407–8. The account in *Letters from a life* includes an excerpt from an interview the Australian artist Sir Sidney Nolan gave to Donald Mitchell (1990) in which Nolan recalls a proposed ballet he and Britten planned in the 1970s in which aspects of Aboriginal and European civilizations were to be juxtaposed. For Britten, it would seem that the tragic story of Dunkerley's suicide was one of the ballet's principal progenitors.

3 The musical language: idiom and structure

1 Quoted in C. Osborne, *Verdi: a life in the theatre*, p. 233. For a discussion of the operatic qualities of the Verdi Requiem, see David Rosen, *Verdi: Requiem* (Cambridge Music Handbooks; Cambridge, 1995).

2 Boyd, 'Britten, Verdi and the Requiem'. For Britten's operatic debt to Verdi, see Cooke and Reed, *Benjamin Britten: 'Billy Budd'*, pp. 161–2, note 24, and Britten's personal tribute to Verdi in *Opera* 2/3 (February 1951).

3 'Mapreading: Benjamin Britten in conversation with Donald Mitchell', in Palmer (ed.), *The Britten companion*, pp. 87–96. The interview took place in February 1969 and was broadcast by the BBC on 10 May 1971, less than one week before the first television transmission of *Owen Wingrave*.

4 Quoted in Osborne, *Verdi*, p. 237. Verdi conducted four performances of his Requiem in London, commencing on 15 May 1875.

5 Boyd, 'Britten, Verdi and the Requiem', p. 3 (Ex. 2).

6 The tenor and baritone soloists who took part in the première and Decca recording of the *War Requiem* were British (Pears) and German (Fischer-Dieskau) respectively. See pp. 26–7.

7 Boyd, 'Britten, Verdi and the Requiem', p. 6.

8 Evans, *The music of Benjamin Britten*, p. 451.

9 This distinctive scoring reflects the continuing influence on Britten of Berg's Violin Concerto, the (posthumous) first performance of which he had attended in Barcelona on 19 April 1936.

10 See Mervyn Cooke, 'Britten and Bali', *Journal of Musicological Research* 7 (1987), pp. 307–39, and notes accompanying the recording of the complete ballet by the London Sinfonietta under Oliver Knussen (Virgin VCD 791103–4, 1990). For a full discussion of the influence of oriental musics on Britten, see the same author's monograph *Britten and the Far East*.

11 Britten reused this technique for identical dramatic reasons in both *Curlew River* (1964) and during the St Mark's scene in *Death in Venice* (1972), a work imbued with gamelan influences on various levels. See Mervyn Cooke, 'Britten and the gamelan: Balinese influences in *Death in Venice*' in Mitchell, *Benjamin Britten: 'Death in Venice'*, pp. 115–28.

12 See Mervyn Cooke, 'Britten and Shakespeare: dramatic and musical cohesion in *A Midsummer Night's Dream*', *Music & Letters* 74/2 (May 1993), pp. 246–68.

13 Evans, *The music of Benjamin Britten*, p. 451.

14 Ibid.

15 Deryck Cooke, *The language of music* (Oxford, 1959), p. 88.

16 Britten chose not to set the Communion text 'Lux aeterna' – which had formed an additional movement in Verdi's Requiem – perhaps because part of it ('et lux perpetua luceat eis') reappears in the course of the 'Libera me'.

17 The tritone C–G flat forms part of the dominant-ninth chord in B flat minor, a harmony already prominently used by Britten at Fig. 1 as if foreshadowing this change of key.

18 Robert Graves noted that shells sounded like musical instruments, making 'a curious singing noise' (*Goodbye to all that*, p. 82).

19 The ashes of the 'Lacrimosa' are recalled by the 'clay' of Owen's text in a parallel which also suggests the famous line from the burial service 'ashes to ashes, dust to dust'.

20 See Eric Roseberry, '"Abraham and Isaac" revisited: reflections on a theme and its inversion' in Reed (ed.), *On Mahler and Britten*, pp. 253–66.

21 Britten composed *Canticle II* immediately after completing *Billy Budd*, and may well have perceived the close similarity between the predicaments of Abraham/Isaac and Captain Vere/Billy Budd. It is intriguing to discover that both Isaac and Billy receive news of their death sentences to sequences of common triads.

22 Palmer (ed.), *The Britten companion*, p. 318. The hypothesis is supported by Michael Kennedy (*Britten*, p. 211). Coincidentally, the vocal score of the *War Requiem* was prepared for publication by Holst's daughter Imogen, then acting as Britten's amanuensis: see p. 24.

23 This procedure again suggests the influence of Berg (cf. note 9 above), who used a twelve-note chord to represent the totality of the universe in his *Altenberg Lieder* (1912).

24 Lest such an interpretation should appear unduly fanciful, it should be noted that Britten generally delights in musical puns of this type. In *Curlew River* (1964), for instance, the only overtly triadic shapes in the entire work occur when the Traveller sings 'I come from the Westland' (Fig. 14). Similarly, Concord's choral dance in *Gloriana* (Act II, scene 1) is entirely composed of concordant harmonies – 'that's the sort of joke one can make, I think', Britten revealed to Imogen Holst shortly after he had written it (see Philip Reed, 'The creative evolution of *Gloriana*' in Paul Banks (ed.), *Britten's 'Gloriana': essays and sources* (Aldeburgh studies in music, No. 1; Woodbridge, 1993), p. 45).

25 The following lines from Owen's poem were inscribed on the poet's tombstone on the instructions of his mother:

> Shall life renew these bodies?
> Of a truth all death will he annul.

In omitting the last three words of the second of those sentences ('all tears assuage?') and thereby turning it into statement rather than question, she completely reversed the negative stance of the poem. See Hibberd, *Wilfred Owen: the last year*, pp. 193–4.

4 Critical reception

1 Peter Evans, 'Britten since the *War Requiem*', *Listener*, 28 May 1964.

2 'Emotion and technique in Britten's *War Requiem*', *The Times*, 11 January 1963. As customary at the time, Mann's article once more appeared anonymously.

3 Fischer-Dieskau, *Echoes of a lifetime*, p. 258.

4 For an account of the Soviet authorities' refusal to allow Vishnevskaya to participate in the early performances of the *War Requiem*, see p. 27.

5 J. Culshaw, *Putting the record straight*, pp. 310–13.

6 'Britten: master composer, man against war', *Daily Mail*, 3 August 1964. The *Evening Standard* had taken similar delight in detailing Britten's income in 1951, on which occasion the journalist concerned had been roundly rebuffed by Donald Mitchell: 'Much of Mr Reid's information gives the impression that he was once Mr Britten's bank manager ... we are even told the price Mr Britten paid for his motor car. Such an extraordinary exposure of any man's private affairs is quite unwarrantable, and, in my experience of musical journalism, the article is without precedent ... In one mouth at least it left a nasty taste.' ('More off than on *Billy Budd*', *Music Survey* 4/2 (February 1952), p. 386; reprinted in Mitchell, *Cradles of the new*, pp. 365–92).

7 Culshaw, *Putting the record straight*, p. 314.

8 Britten, *On receiving the first Aspen award*, p. 11.

9 *The Times*, 13 December 1963.

10 See the lengthy reviews published in the *Japan Times* (1 March 1965) and *Asahi Evening News* (24 February 1965).

11 Letter from Britten to David Adams, 27 November 1965. A pirated edition of the *War Requiem* was published in the USSR (which was not a signatory to the Berne Convention governing international copyright restrictions) in 1968.

12 Dean Wallace, 'A moving rendition of Britten's *War Requiem*', *San Francisco Chronicle*, 8 December 1964.

13 Reviews by Martin Cooper (*Daily Telegraph*, 10 January 1963) and Joan Chissell (*The Times*, 20 January 1972). The 1972 performance took place at the Royal Festival Hall.

14 *Evening Standard*, 3 December 1951. See Mitchell, *Cradles of the New*, pp. 368–71.

15 Igor Stravinsky and Robert Craft, *Themes and Conclusions* (London, 1972), pp. 26–7.

16 Review by Martin Cooper, *Daily Telegraph*, 10 January 1963. Twenty-three years later, Alan Blyth wrote in the same newspaper (2 December 1986) of Vishnevskaya's performance under Simon Rattle at the Royal Opera House in memory of Pears, who had died earlier in the year: 'No more as long-breathed as she used to be, she sometimes had to struggle to sustain her phrases, but the iron-willed conviction and peculiarly plangent timbre that have always informed her singing of the Latin text were even more unforgettably individual than in the past.'

17 An identical problem has been encountered more recently in the case of Steven Spielberg's masterly depiction of the horrors of the holocaust in his film *Schindler's List* (Universal, 1993). Recipient of seven Academy Awards (including one for its superbly crafted score by John Williams), the film is rightly regarded by many as a cinematographic masterpiece. But for those who disagree with this assessment, the film's highly emotive subject-matter will always be an unfortunate source of critical ammunition.

18 Carpenter, *Britten*, p. 410.

19 'Britten's craft and vision', *Sunday Times*, 13 January 1963.

20 *The Times*, 20 January 1972.

21 See Lesley Garner, 'Britten and the pity of war', *Daily Telegraph*, 3 August 1991.

22 'War and eroticism', *Listener*, 13 February 1986.

23 Kennedy, *Britten*, pp. 213–14.

24 'The two worlds of modernism', *Observer*, 3 June 1962.

25 *Time & Tide*, 7 June 1962.

26 'Question of faith', *Daily Telegraph*, 8 August 1964.

27 'Britten's symbolic Requiem, symbolically played', *New York Times*, 23 May 1992. Controversy again surrounded the work in New York in 1995, when an article by Alex Ross entitled 'In music, though, there were no victories' (*New York Times*, 20 August) explored the extraordinary sentiment that 'a work so steeped in the philosophy of pacifism is sadly inappropriate to the circumstances of World War II'. Ross's article generated a heated debate in the newspaper's correspondence column when a letter from Burton Caine published on 10 September proclaimed that Britten had wilfully ignored the attempted liquidation of the Jewish race, having concerned himself only with the plight of soldiers from Britain, Germany and Russia; citing Owen's 'Parable of the Old Man and the Young' as if the words had been written by the composer himself, Caine surmised that 'the message is one of exultation of Christianity and contempt for Judaism. This is grim news after the Holocaust.' Such a perverse misinterpretation could not go unchallenged, and the record was set straight on 8 October when a letter from Arthur Shippee roundly rebuffed Caine's short-sightedness and curtly concluded 'it is grim news if such a bizarre charge gains any currency'. I am grateful to Donald Mitchell and David Drew for drawing this correspondence to my attention.

28 'Benjamin Britten: tributes and memories', *Tempo* 120 (1977), pp. 5–6. Holloway concluded, however, that '[Britten's] music has the power to connect the avant-garde with the lost paradise of tonality; it conserves and renovates in the boldest and simplest manner; it shows how old usages can be refreshed and remade, and how the new can be saved from mere rootlessness, etiolation, lack of connexion and communication.'

29 Alan Blyth, 'Tribute to Pears', *Daily Telegraph*, 2 December 1986.

30 Plomer's essay on the *War Requiem* first appeared in the booklet accompanying Britten's Decca recording, and was reprinted in the programme book to the Pears memorial concert at Covent Garden on 30 November 1986.

31 See Martyn Harry's essay on Jarman's film in *Music and Musicians* (January 1989), pp. 14–17.

32 Quoted in 'Battle of Britten', *Radio Times*, 18–24 March 1989.

33 'How a cinematic eye sees beyond the script', *Sunday Times*, 8 January 1989. The BBC

(which commissioned the film) had warned that the content should not be too explicitly violent, a stipulation which may have conditioned Jarman's restrained approach.

34 *The Times*, 5 January 1989.
35 *Music and Musicians* (January 1989), p. 17.
36 Undated cutting from the *Manchester Guardian* (November 1963), Britten–Pears Library.

Select bibliography

Boyd, Malcolm, 'Britten, Verdi and the Requiem', *Tempo* 86 (1968), pp. 2–6

Brett, Philip (ed.), *Benjamin Britten: 'Peter Grimes'* (Cambridge Opera Handbooks, 1983)

Britten, Benjamin, *On receiving the first Aspen award* (London, 1964)

Carpenter, Humphrey, *Benjamin Britten: a biography* (London, 1992)

Cooke, Mervyn, *Britten and the Far East* (Aldeburgh studies in music, No. 4; Woodbridge, 1997)

Cooke, Mervyn and Reed, Philip, *Benjamin Britten: 'Billy Budd'* (Cambridge Opera Handbooks, 1993)

Culshaw, John, *Putting the record straight* (London, 1981)

Duncan, Ronald, *Working with Britten* (Welcombe, 1981)

Evans, Peter, 'Britten's *War Requiem*', *Tempo* 61–2 (Spring–Summer 1962), pp. 20–39

  The music of Benjamin Britten (London, 1979; second edition, 1989)

Fischer-Dieskau, Dietrich, *Echoes of a lifetime*, trans. Ruth Hein (London, 1989)

Graves, Robert, *Goodbye to all that* (London, 1929; revised edition 1957)

Gurney, Ivor, *Ivor Gurney: war letters*, ed. R. K. R. Thornton (London, 1983)

Hibberd, Dominic, 'Concealed messages in Wilfred Owen's trench letters', *Notes and Queries* 27/6 (December 1980), p. 531

  Wilfred Owen: the last year (London, 1992)

Jarman, Derek, *War Requiem: the film* (London, 1989)

Kennedy, Michael, *Britten* ('Master Musicians', London, 1981; second edition, 1993)

Mitchell, Donald, *Britten and Auden in the Thirties: the year 1936* (London, 1981)

  Cradles of the new: writings on music 1951–91, selected by Christopher Palmer, edited by Mervyn Cooke (London, 1995)

Mitchell, Donald (ed.), *Benjamin Britten: 'Death in Venice'* (Cambridge Opera Handbooks, 1987)

Mitchell, Donald, and Reed, Philip, *Letters from a life: selected letters and diaries of Benjamin Britten 1913–76*, volumes I and II (London, 1991)

Osborne, Charles, *Verdi: a life in the theatre* (London, 1987)

Owen, Harold, *Journey from obscurity*, three volumes (London, 1963–5); abridged edition, ed. Hilary M. Gornall, one volume (Oxford, 1968)

Owen, Wilfred, *The collected poems of Wilfred Owen*, ed. C. Day Lewis (London, 1963)

The poems of Wilfred Owen, ed. with a Memoir and notes by E. Blunden (London, 1955)

The poems of Wilfred Owen, ed. J. Stallworthy (London, 1990)

Wilfred Owen: selected letters, ed. J. Bell (Oxford, 1985)

Palmer, Christopher (ed.), *The Britten companion* (London, 1984)

Reed, Philip (ed.), *On Mahler and Britten: essays in honour of Donald Mitchell on his 70th birthday* (Aldeburgh studies in music, No. 3; Woodbridge, 1995)

Schafer, Murray, *British composers in interview* (London, 1964)

Stallworthy, Jon, *Wilfred Owen: a biography* (Oxford, 1974)

Vishnevskaya, Galina, *Galina: a Russian story* (London, 1984)

White, Eric Walter, *Benjamin Britten: his life and operas*, second edition ed. John Evans (London, 1983)

Whittall, Arnold, 'Tonal instability in Britten's *War Requiem*', *Music Review* 24 (August 1963), pp. 201–4

Index